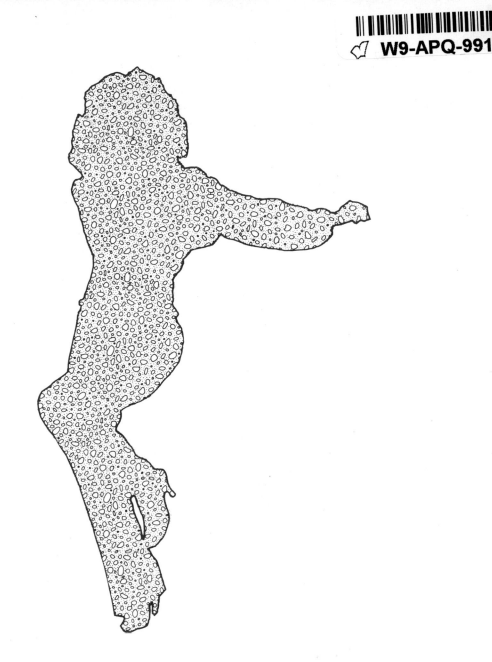

THE COMPLETE GUIDE TO
DISCO DANCING

THE COM
DISCO

by Karen Lu
Photography by
Chart Illustrations by Robert

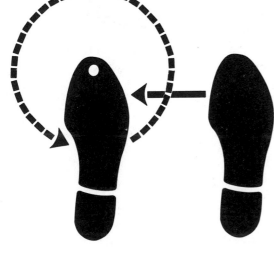

LETE GUIDE TO
DANCING

stgarten

ernie Lustgarten

ohin and David Gentry

WARNER **W** **BOOKS**

THIS BOOK IS DEDICATED
with love and appreciation to
Bernie Lustgarten, Marc Richardson, my dear parents,
and all my students.

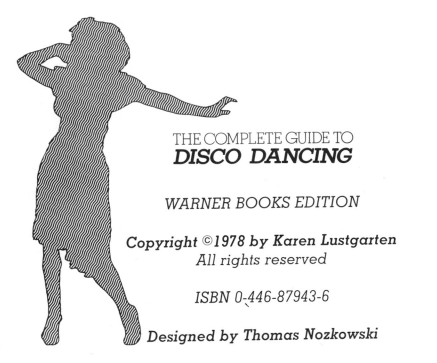

THE COMPLETE GUIDE TO
DISCO DANCING

WARNER BOOKS EDITION

Copyright ©1978 by Karen Lustgarten
All rights reserved

ISBN 0-446-87943-6

Designed by Thomas Nozkowski

Warner Books, Inc., 75 Rockefeller Plaza, New York, N.Y. 10019

A Warner Communications Company

Printed in the United States of America

Not associated with Warner Press, Inc., of Anderson, Indiana

First Printing: October, 1978

10 9 8 7 6 5

ACKNOWLEDGMENTS

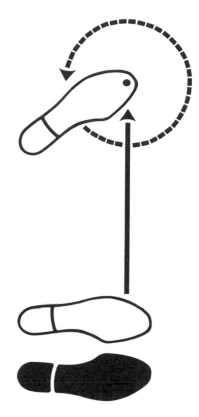

How can I thank Bernie Lustgarten, my former husband and my best friend, who over the years has also become my talented photographer, concerned adviser, and keen research assistant. I am grateful for his wonderful name and his devoted friendship.

I am also grateful to my dear friend Marc Richardson, a multitalented visionary who has been my disco DJ and "grand vizier" regarding the "biz."

Appreciation extends to John and Ilene Medovich, who have always believed in me and helped me through some difficult times.

My parents deserve words of thanks for all the "thousands" of dollars they kid about having spent on my early dance lessons. None of it was wasted!

Phyllis Benowitz, my super secretary, deserves a special acknowledgment. It is partly due to her efficiency, dependability, and sense of responsibility that I've been able to maintain sanity during these hectic times.

Thank you, my three handsome partners in Chapter IV: Ivan Ladizinsky, Dr. Robert Illa, and Sonny Harper.

I'd also like to express appreciation to the staff at St. Tropez Hair Design, San Francisco, for their very fine hair care and styling. Thanks to Bullocks Northern California (Stonestown) for the loan of most of the shoes; the pants in steps E, G, N, and O; and the top in steps H and I.

CONTENTS

PROLOGUE by Ivan Ladizinsky

There was a time when the local radio station would send out one of its disc jockeys to a high school gym with turntables, amplifiers, speakers, and a microphone to provide the music for a Friday night sock hop. That goes back more than thirty years. Around the country there are still towns where teenagers take off their shoes and whirl around a waxed and polished gymnasium floor, exercising their youth to the rhythms of the "tops in pops." In those early days the popular dance was the Lindy hop and later, the Twist. Ballroom dancing was still acceptable and the Samba was particularly popular.

Now, we "Hustle" at the disco. Surrounded by frenetic flashing lights, electric images reflecting from mirrored walls, and sparkling ceilings, we step, shuffle, prance, and undulate to the irresistible beat of disco music. It pulsates at us from every direction over marvelously engineered sound systems. The audio and visual experience lifts us out of ourselves and it is not just our bodies that are moved, but our souls.

Discotheques, as we know and love them today, probably had their seeds sown on the floor of some forgotten Paris bistro whose owner cleared a place one magic night so his customers might dance to the current hit playing on a Phillips phonograph propped up on the bar by Cinzano ash trays. Disco has come a long way, baby, and from New York to San Francisco, the night life for millions of happy people throbs to the one hundred twenty beats per minute that is the heart of disco music. Fashions, shoes, cosmetics, an entire lifestyle has evolved around the spirit of disco. It's a free-style way of going—very easy and very open.

There is nothing subtle about disco music or dancing to it. It is comprised of a feeling of rock, a taste of jazz, afro and latin rhythms, adaptations from Tchaikovsky's Romeo and Juliet to the theme from *Star Wars*. Disco treatments of all kinds of music gets people from fifteen to fifty on their feet, moving more freely than ever before. Disco dancing is more expressive than any preceding type of social dancing. It allows for a great deal of individuality, but there are disciplines. There are steps and style. *Style* is the key, and by learning a few basic steps and turns, the individual can develop a personal style with precision and polish. Disco dancing, partner style, is also the rage and it takes a well-matched twosome to make it fun and glamorous.

The most exciting and accomplished pioneer of disco dancing on the West Coast is Karen Lustgarten. Karen teaches hundreds of enthusiastic disco-neophytes of greatly varying ages every week. Karen is a dynamic, beautiful, and joyous instructor who makes the learning process fun and easy. After her lesson, a previously uninitiated group of people will be having the time of their lives dancing with élan and a good-time smile to a feverish disco beat. Many of Karen's former students have taken her dances and gone on to become instructors themselves. This book brings you the best of the best. Karen Lustgarten and her most popular disco dances that make anyone look good on the dance floor...dedicated to all you happy Hustlers.

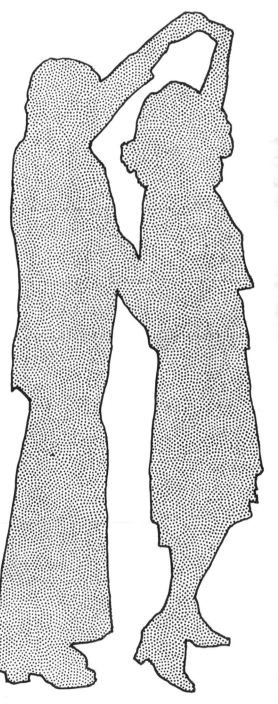

PROLOGUE

INTRODUCTION

When I first began teaching disco dancing in March, 1973 no one knew what the word "disco" meant. So I changed the name of my class to "fad" dancing and I described it as the kind of dancing you do when you're at a house party or a nightclub that plays popular music. My first students were young adults who wanted to look coordinated and feel confident about "fast" dancing in any social situation. Everyone who places themselves on a dance floor is automatically on display, and my "fad" dance students wanted to place their best foot forward!

Practically no one was teaching this kind of dancing when I started, so I had to devise my own way of translating seemingly amorphous writhing into something that made dance sense to my students. I had studied ballet and jazz since childhood, and had developed a knack for learning steps and style quickly just by observing other dancers. With notebook and pen in hand, I'd haunt the precious few discotheques and nightclubs around town to watch dancers; or I'd study a group of high school kids at a "social." Later I went to Los Angeles and New York for more notetaking. For awhile I felt like an intruding anthropologist observing restless natives around the flickering lights of an electric campfire.

I didn't realize it then, but what I was really doing was researching a dance form that had never been studied or written about before. By faithfully recording popular dances and breaking them down into steps, variations, and style, I was proving that disco dancing can be articulated, and can therefore be taught. My notebook grew and the number of students increased. Word was out that a hesitant, self-conscious beginner could learn how to "fast" dance by taking fast dance lessons! In time I developed and refined a teaching technique that gave every student a pair of new dancing feet and a good-time smile.

This book represents the distillation of my five and one half years of researching, notetaking, and teaching disco dancing. The popularity of the individual dances and their names may change from year to year, but the basic steps remain constant.

I have written this book with a twofold purpose in mind. I'm hoping that by taking the threat, stigma, or mystique out of disco dancing, these pages will inspire the previously uninitiated to get their feet wet, so to speak, and discover the pure joy that is disco dancing. I also hope this book will help to legitimize disco dancing as a unique and liberating dance form that makes you smile.

Karen Lustgarten
San Francisco, 1978

INTRODUCTION

CHAPTER ONE

PREPARING YOU THE DISCO DAN

People who wouldn't dream of running a marathon are now putting themselves through a nonstop cardiovascular stamina test on the dance floor. Disco dancing is not exactly a frivolous form of physical activity. Once you admit yourself into a disco, you've surrendered your body for the night. You become anesthetized by the spirits, hypnotized by the electronics, and mesmerized by the continuous music. The wonderful Wizards of Oz in the DJ booth know just how to manipulate the infectious polyrhythmic sounds to entice the unsuspecting into hysterical exhaustion. Any effects from a night at the disco are usually felt the following morning in the form of temporary paralysis.

Don't kid yourself, disco dancing *is* exercise! It requires all the stamina, strength, and flexibility that any other sport demands; and if you're smart, you'll condition for it much like a football player during preseason training. To avoid any after-effects, you should create your own little conditioning program that improves your strength, flexibility, and cardiovascular stamina.

Besides being in condition, disco dancing also requires a combination of skillful, graceful movements that are at once loose and controlled. You'll notice that the feet stay fairly close together and the dancing is done in a relatively small space. But the steps are always dressed up in "style" to give them a disco "look." "Style" means the individual way you coordinate your feet, hips, shoulders, knees, arms, head, and midriff. Quality of

BODY FOR
E EXPERIENCE

style varies among dancers depending on their skill, grace, personality, and interpretation of the music.

Some dance with a fluid, subtle, sexy style. Others prefer to be flamboyant and acrobatic. Gone forever is the spasmodic, uncoordinated, convulsive "style" of the psychedelic 60's. Disco dancing is a form of self-expression, but there *is* a skill and discipline to it.

I recommend that you begin by loosening and isolating the movement in different parts of your body. Put on your favorite high energy disco record and isolate your body parts in rhythm. Bounce your knees, swing your arms freely, lean over from side to side, lift your shoulders one at a time, tilt your head in all directions, sway your hips, and push out your ribcage to either side. Try to isolate the parts separately for awhile, then combine a few of them. The idea is to release any tension and stiffness from your body first, then to move the separate parts *before* you ever take your first step.

Initially disco movements will feel awkward and incongruous. After all, we're not accustomed to moving this way in normal life. But with consistent practice you'll become more comfortable, your body will loosen, and your dancing will take on more style. Soon you'll become addicted to the disco dance experience: a happy, energetic dance form that puts you in an ebullient mood and leaves your body and soul bathed in a warm, wet glow.

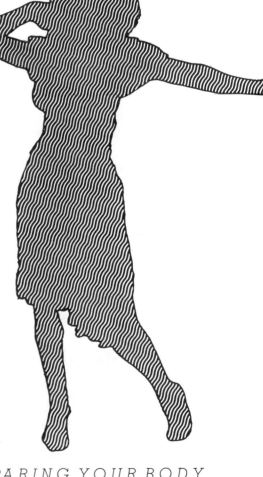

PREPARING YOUR BODY

CHAPTER TWO

THE BASIC DISC AND DANCES

This chapter contains the basic vocabulary you'll need to learn the "art" of disco dancing. True, there are many disco steps and dances other than those presented in this chapter, but you'll discover that most of them are mutations and variations.

The chapter opens with the easiest steps and dances. You'll want to practice the steps first until you feel comfortable with them and can do them with "style," before trying one of the dances. For the sake of simplicity, I've presented most steps starting with the right (R) foot. All of these dances are done facing, but not touching your partner. Usually it doesn't matter on which side you begin, so if you prefer to start left, feel free. You'll notice that at times the feet play a secondary role to the hips and arms—disco dancing is a "shaky" business. The idea is to develop some skill, then keep it all moving.

To help you with the counts, I've added a rhythm chart for each step. Keep in mind that not all disco music is written in 4/4 time, nor should you expect to be stepping on only quarter notes. But you will notice that every recommended record has a steady, consistent beat. Use the beats and accents in the music to help you count out your steps. Almost automatically you'll step on the beats and accents that are most comfortable for dancing, and you'll feel right in time with the rhythm. The practice music I've recommended consists mostly of

STEPS

disco classics (or cuts that may become classics in the near future). Admittedly, a few are just personal favorites. By all means, if you have favorite disco music not recommended in these pages, then please try the steps to your own disco records!

One of the unique and most attractive aspects of disco dancing is that you and your partner are not required to perform the same dance together, or to perform only one dance to one record. Since you're not touching each other, you have complete freedom to perform any of the steps, styles, and variations that your little feet desire. For example, you and your partner may decide to start with the same dance, then break off into different dances. Or you may want to start differently, or you may decide to always do the same dance, but change your dances frequently before the record ends. The beauty of disco dancing is that once you learn the basics, the variety of combinations is limited only by your imagination. Let yourself go!

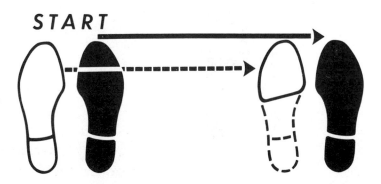

GLOSSARY

STEP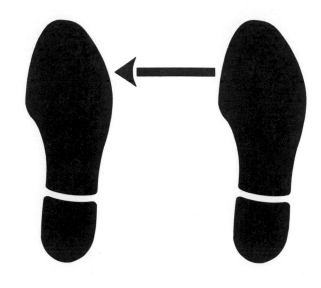

TOUCH

LIFT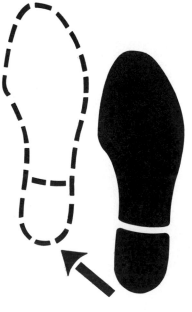

SPIN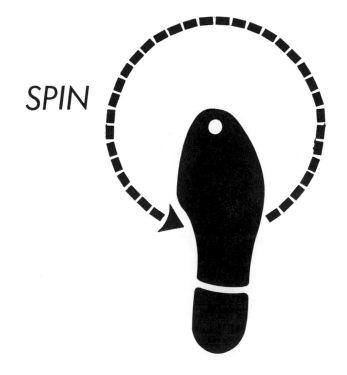

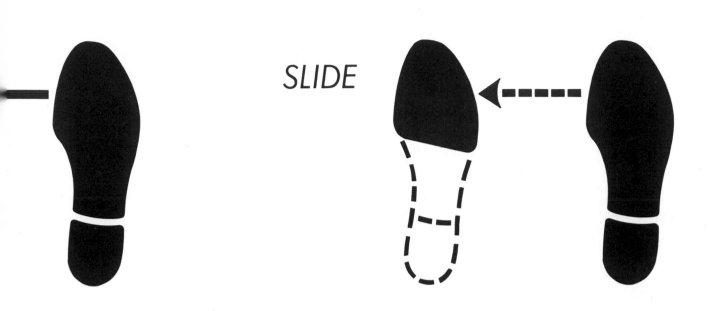

SLIDE

PIVOT

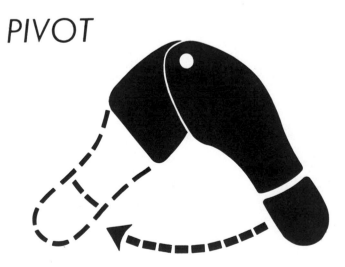

SHUFFLE

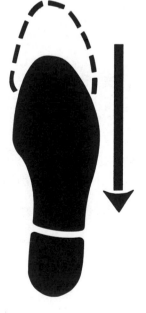

Here it is, the easiest and most basic of all disco dance steps. Use this one as a transition between more complicated steps, or as a respite when you find yourself losing stamina on the dance floor.

A. *THE SINGLE TOUCH STEP*

Start Position: feet together

Counts	Description
1	Touch (tap) your R foot out to R side and swing your arms apart
2	Step R foot next to the L one (close) and swing arms together in front of your body
3	Touch L foot out to the L side and swing arms apart
4	Step L foot next to R one (close) and swing arms together

(So far so good?)

Style

The feeling is bouncy; the knees are loose; and one hip can swing out a bit when you touch one foot sideways. Repeat the step several times continuously until it feels comfortable, then add the variations. Have fun with it!

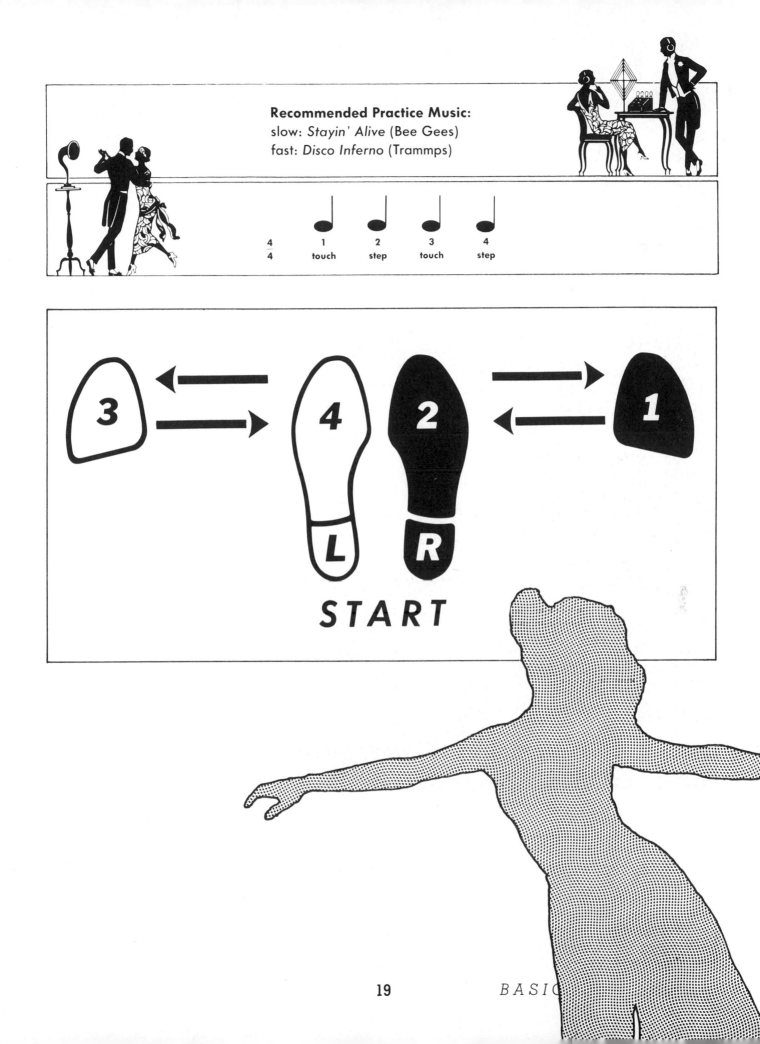

Recommended Practice Music:
slow: *Stayin' Alive* (Bee Gees)
fast: *Disco Inferno* (Trammps)

$\frac{4}{4}$ 1 touch   2 step   3 touch   4 step

START

BASI

THE SINGLE TOUCH STEP: **VARIATIONS**

FORWARD VARIATION:
On the 1st count, tap the R forward and swing the arms backward; on the 3rd count, tap the L foot forward and swing arms backward. For a bit more style, push your pelvis forward each time the foot taps forward.

BACKWARD VARIATION:
You can keep your feet a little further apart on this variation. On the 1st count, tap the R behind the L foot; on the 3rd count, tap the L foot slightly behind the R. Let both arms swing backward or let them swing across your body (one in front, the other in back)

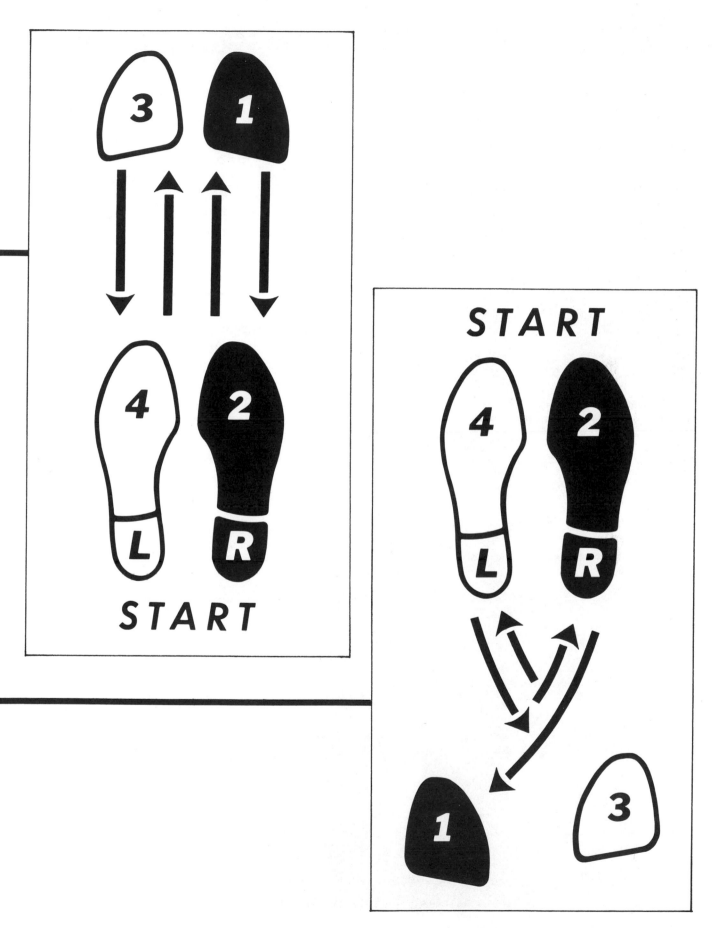

BASIC DISCO STEPS

B. THE DOUBLE TOUCH STEP

Start Position: Feet together

Counts	Description
1	Touch (tap) R foot out to the side and swing your arms apart
2	Touch R foot in, next to the L foot and swing arms together (in front of your body)
3	Repeat count 1
4	Step R foot next to the L one (close) and swing arms together

Reverse to the left side:

5	Touch L out to the L side and swing arms out
6	Touch L foot close to R and swing arms together (or crossed in front of body)
7	Repeat count 5
8	Step L foot next to R (close) and swing arms together

Style:

Keep your knees loose and a bit bouncy, and let your hips move out and in with your foot. Repeat the step R and L as often as you like without pausing.

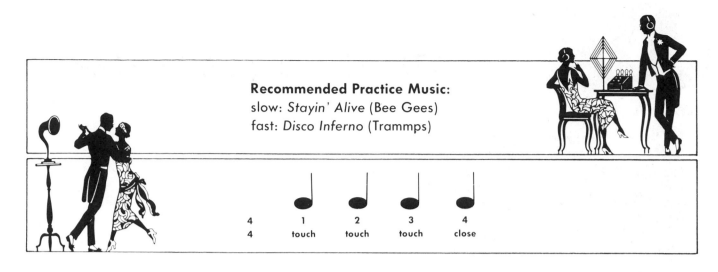

Recommended Practice Music:
slow: *Stayin' Alive* (Bee Gees)
fast: *Disco Inferno* (Trammps)

4	1	2	3	4
4	touch	touch	touch	close

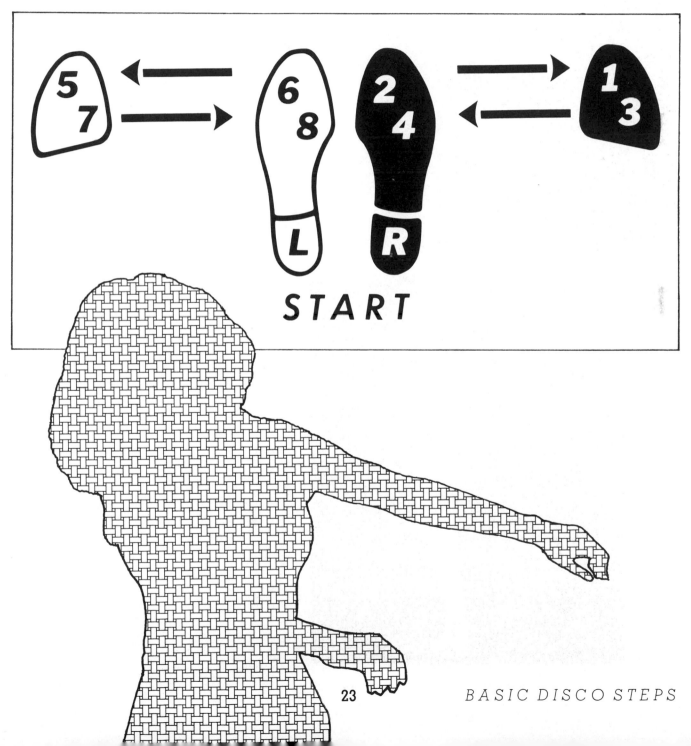

START

BASIC DISCO STEPS

THE DOUBLE TOUCH STEP: **VARIATIONS**

FORWARD VARIATION:
On the 1st and 3rd counts, tap the R foot forward and let your arms swing backward behind your hips (on counts 5 and 7 tap L backward).

BACK CROSS VARIATION:
On the 1st and 3rd counts touch the R foot behind the L one. Let one arm swing in front of your body while the other swings in back. Repeat on the L side (L foot touches behind the R one on counts 5 and 7).

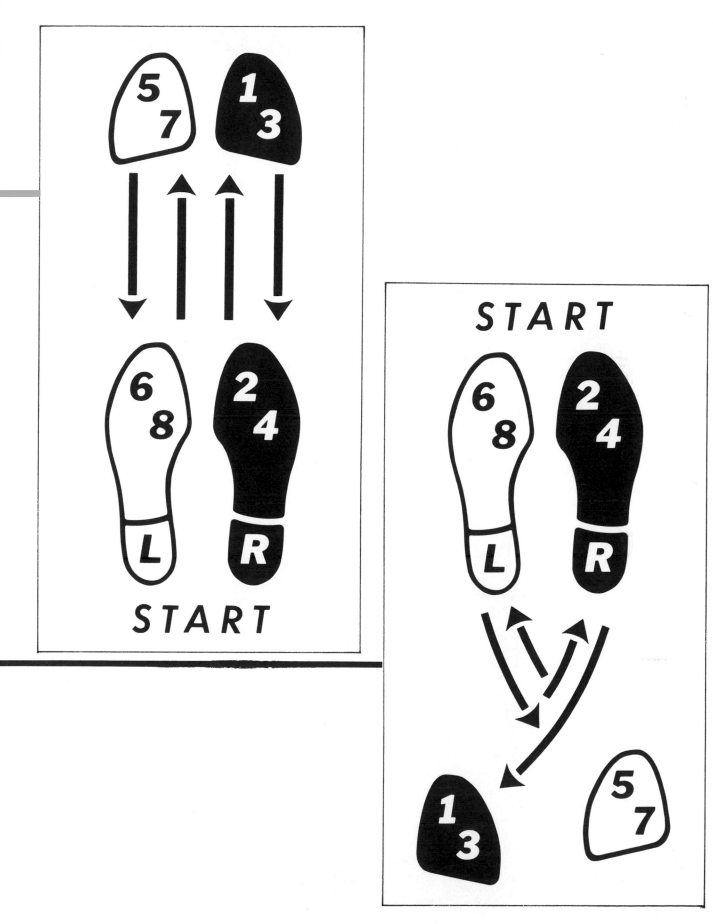

BASIC DISCO STEPS

DANCE: #1:   *The Disco Dynosoar*

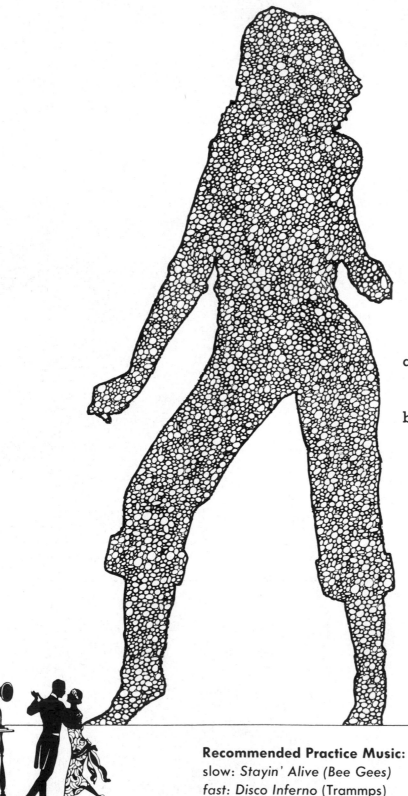

Here it is, the most basic of the disco dances. This one combines two basic steps: the Single Touch and the Double Touch steps. Try dancing the below dance pattern without pausing and without losing a beat when you change direction from sideways to forward to backward. Keep the pattern moving for as long as you like until it feels easy and comfortable, then make up your own pattern based on these two steps (and put some style into it). Good luck!

Pattern

a   Double Touch Step to R and L side

b   Single Touch Step (twice sideways)

Repeat the above, dancing the forward then backward variations.

Recommended Practice Music:
slow: *Stayin' Alive* (Bee Gees)
fast: *Disco Inferno* (Trammps)

BASIC DISCO STEPS

This is another very basic, easy disco step used mostly as a transition between more complicated steps. Be sure to put lots of style and pzazz into all of the variations, too.

C. THE SINGLE SLIDE STEP

Start Position: feet together

Counts	Description
1	Step your R foot to the R side and really put your weight on it. Let your R knee bend as you dip your upper body to the R when you take this step.
2	Slide your L foot next to the R one and straighten up (but don't stiffen up). There's no weight on the L foot.
3	Repeat count one to the L side (step L foot to side)
4	Repeat count 2 with the R foot (slide the R foot next to the L ONE)

Style

Keep practicing this step from R to L until it feels and looks smooth. Exaggerate the step to the side by bending the knee lower.

There are several different ways to stylize this step, only one of which is to bend the knee and dip over. Another popular style is to twist your upper body very slightly when you step (twist to the L slightly when stepping R; twist R when stepping L).

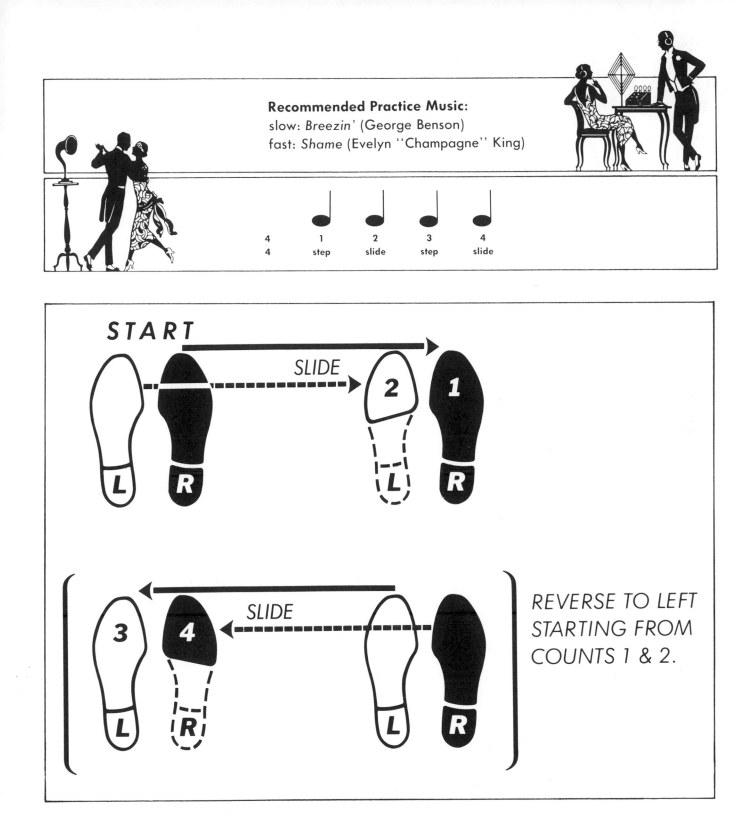

Recommended Practice Music:
slow: *Breezin'* (George Benson)
fast: *Shame* (Evelyn "Champagne" King)

4	1	2	3	4
4	step	slide	step	slide

START

SLIDE

SLIDE

REVERSE TO LEFT
STARTING FROM
COUNTS 1 & 2.

BASIC DISCO STEPS

THE SINGLE SLIDE STEP: **VARIATIONS**

LIFT VARIATION:
On the *2nd and 4th* counts, instead of sliding your foot along the floor, lift it by lifting your knee and bringing it close to or behind the standing leg. Let your arms swing freely across your body. As long as the standing knee is never stiff, you'll be O.K.

SPIN VARIATION:
On the *4th count*, spin around to the L on the ball of your L foot so that you've made a 360° turn in one count. Try the spin only occasionally at first, lest you become too dizzy!

FORWARD BACKWARD VARIATION:
On *count 1*, step forward on your R and lean forward slightly. On *count 3*, step backward on the L foot and dip back a bit.

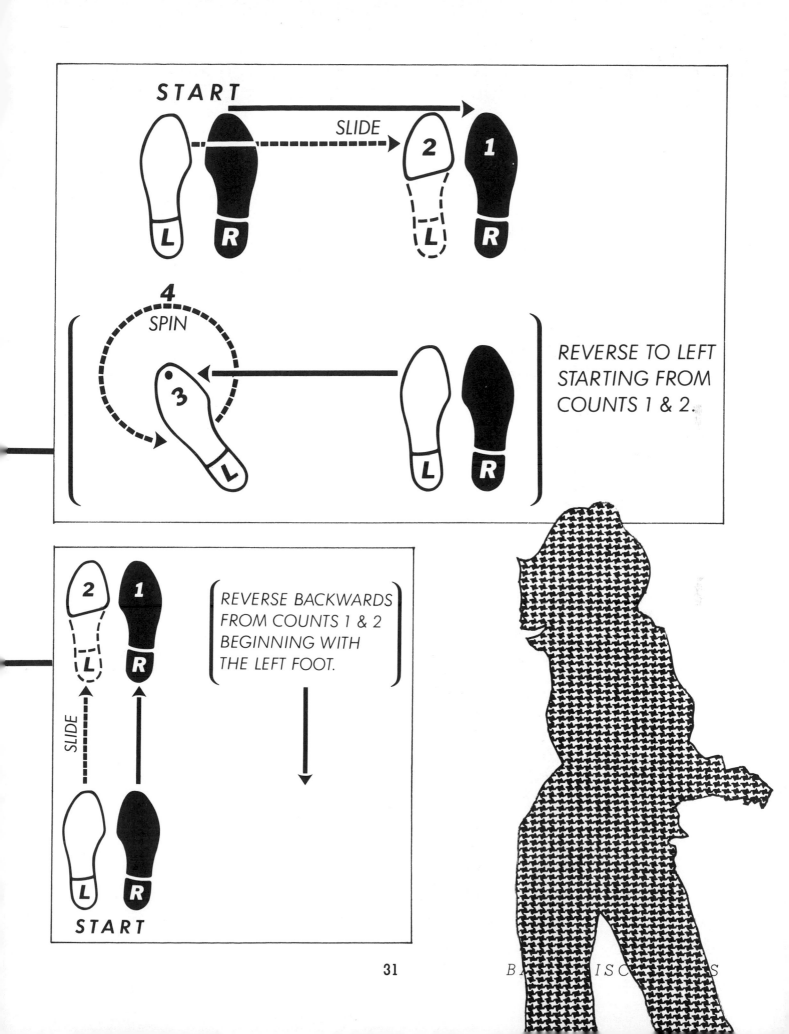

START

SLIDE

2   1
L   R

L   R

4
SPIN

3
L

REVERSE TO LEFT
STARTING FROM
COUNTS 1 & 2.

L   R

2   1
L   R

REVERSE BACKWARDS
FROM COUNTS 1 & 2
BEGINNING WITH
THE LEFT FOOT.

SLIDE

L   R

START

Of all the basic disco steps, the double slide is probably the one most frequently used on the disco dance floor. Done side to side or forward and back, you'll find this step incorporated somewhere in the choreography of most disco dances. If you practice the basic step, then add all the variations without pausing, you'll be creating your own dance comprised of just this double slide.

D.   *THE DOUBLE SLIDE STEP*

Start Position: feet together

Counts	Description
1	Step R foot to the R side
2	Slide (or step) L foot next to the R one
3	Repeat count 1
4	Tap (touch) L foot next to R immediately reverse to the L side:
5	Step L foot to L side
6	Slide (or step) R foot next to the L one
7	Repeat count 5 (step L foot to L side)
8	Tap (touch) R foot next to the L one

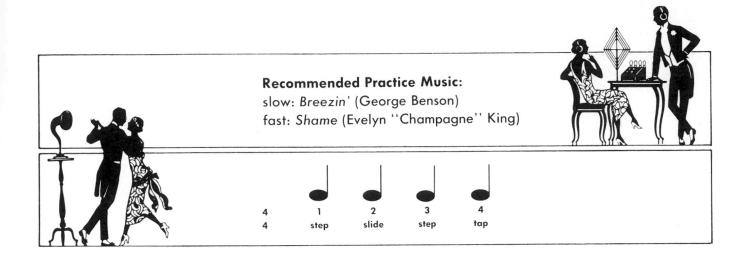

Recommended Practice Music:
slow: *Breezin'* (George Benson)
fast: *Shame* (Evelyn ''Champagne'' King)

4	1	2	3	4
4	step	slide	step	tap

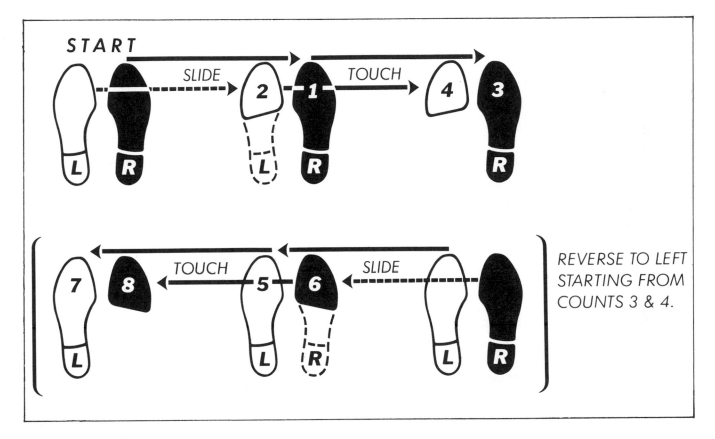

START

SLIDE   TOUCH

2   1   4   3

L   R   L   R   R

TOUCH   SLIDE

7   8   5   6

L   L   R   L   R

*REVERSE TO LEFT
STARTING FROM
COUNTS 3 & 4.*

Style

After the footwork feels comfortable and smooth, add a dip by leaning over slightly to the R when you step to the R side on counts 1 and 3 (dip L on counts 5 & 7 stepping to the L). Let your arms swing freely and loosely from side to side on each count. Later you can try swinging them in the opposite direction from the side you're stepping toward. The feeling is bouncy in the knees, free swinging in the arms.

BASIC DISCO STEPS

THE DOUBLE SLIDE STEP: **VARIATIONS**

LIFT VARIATION

On the *4th count*, instead of tapping the L foot, lift it slightly from the knee close to or behind your standing L leg (when heading to the L side, lift the R foot on the 8th count)

SPIN VARIATION:

On the *4th count*, spin around to the R on the ball of your R foot so that you've made a 360° turn in one count (when heading L, spin to the L on the ball of your L foot on the 8th count). Try the spin only occasionally at first.

CROSS VARIATION:

On the *2nd count*, cross the L foot over the R (when starting to the R side); or cross the R foot over the L on the 6th count (when moving to the L)

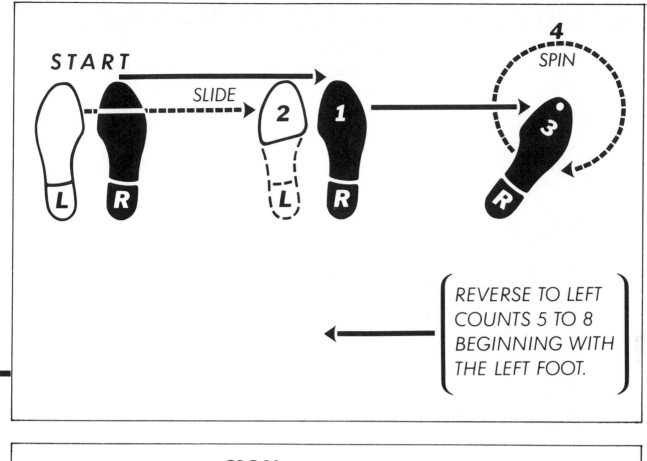

START

SLIDE

4
SPIN

REVERSE TO LEFT COUNTS 5 TO 8 BEGINNING WITH THE LEFT FOOT.

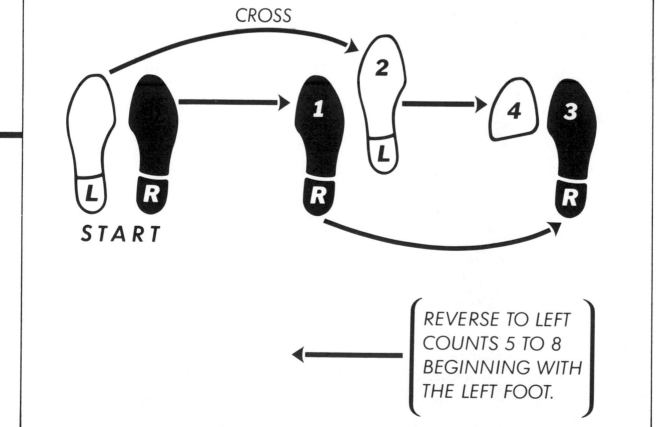

CROSS

START

REVERSE TO LEFT COUNTS 5 TO 8 BEGINNING WITH THE LEFT FOOT.

BASIC DISCO STEPS

THE DOUBLE SLIDE STEP: **VARIATIONS**

FORWARD/BACKWARD VARIATION:

Counts	Description
1	Step forward on your R foot and lean your upper body forward slightly
2	Slide (or step) the L foot forward to meet the R one and straighten your upper body
3	Repeat count 1
4	Repeat count 2

Immediately repeat the step heading backward:

5	Step the L foot backward and lean back slightly at the same time
6	Slide (or step) the R foot backward and next to the L one
7	Repeat count 5
8	Repeat count 6

TURN VARIATIONS (TRAVELS SIDEWAYS):

Counts	Description
1	Step R to side and face your body toward the R side, anticipating a R turn
2	Cross L foot over R and pivot around (360°) on L
3	Step R out to side
4	Touch L next to R

This variation may also be reversed to the L.

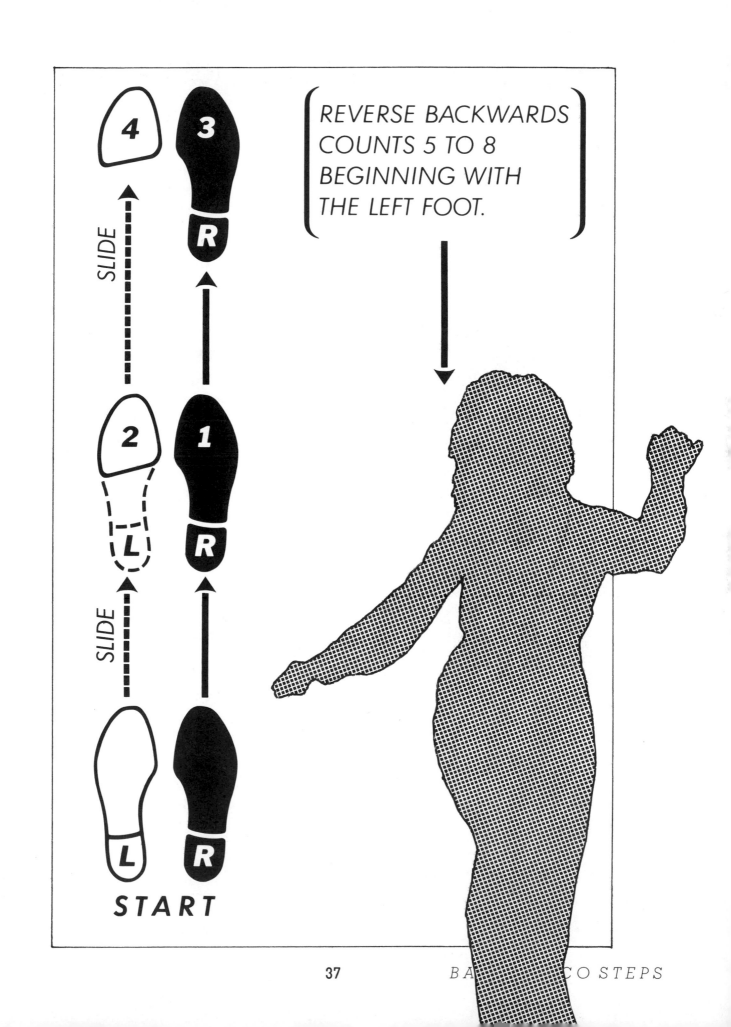

REVERSE BACKWARDS COUNTS 5 TO 8 BEGINNING WITH THE LEFT FOOT.

4

3 R

SLIDE

2

1 R

L

SLIDE

L

R

START

DANCE #2   THE ROLLER COASTER

Now you can combine the Slide Steps into a simple and very popular disco dance known as the Roller Coaster. Like all disco dances, you don't pause for coffee and donuts between steps and their variations; they all flow together like the music, without beginning or end.

Pattern

a   Double Slide Step to the R and L sides

b   Double Slide Step with the lift or spin variation

c   Slide Step with the lift or spin variation

Forward/Backward: Repeat the above pattern dancing the forward then the backward variations without pausing between changes in direction. The pattern continues in a cycle for as long as the music (or your stamina) lasts. Once you've mastered this pattern and can dance it with lots of style, make up your own combinations from these two Slide Steps and their variations. Let your feet go, and see what they can do!

Recommended Practice Music:
slow: *Breezin'* (George Benson)
fast: *Shame* (Evelyn ''Champagne'' King)

E. THE CROSS STEP

Start Position: Feet together

Counts	Description
1	Step R foot forward
2	Cross L over R and put your weight on the L foot (lean forward slightly on to the L foot)
3	Step R foot back
4	Tap L foot next to R
	Then immediately repeat on L side
5	Step L foot forward
6	Cross R over L and put weight on R foot
7	Step L foot back
8	Tap R foot next to L

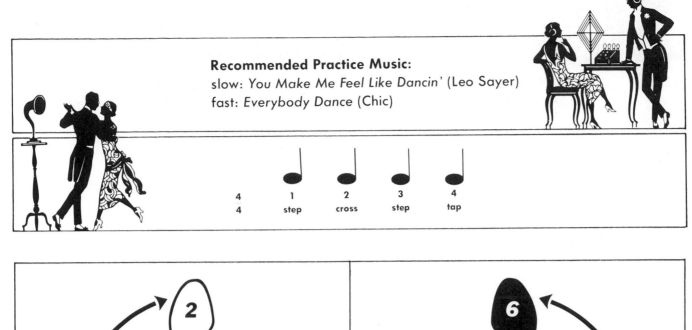

Recommended Practice Music:
slow: *You Make Me Feel Like Dancin'* (Leo Sayer)
fast: *Everybody Dance* (Chic)

4	1	2	3	4
4	step	cross	step	tap

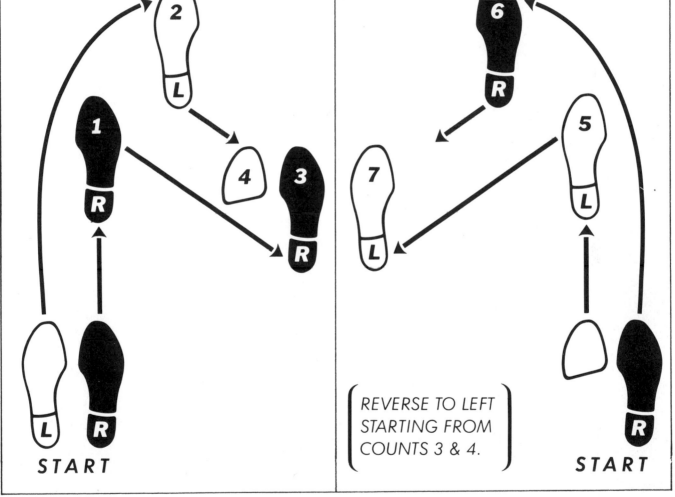

REVERSE TO LEFT STARTING FROM COUNTS 3 & 4.

DANCE #3:   THE SPECIAL K

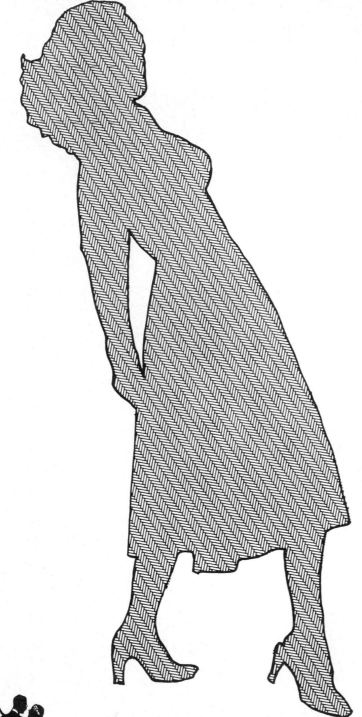

This dance is a bit more complicated because it combines more steps from the previous pages: the Double Slide, the Double Touch, the Cross, and the Slide Steps. Try the below pattern first then add the variations. After you feel comfortable with this pattern, make up your own combination in any order you like, based on these 4 steps. Surprise yourself! Remember, no rest periods between sections; when you finish the pattern, start all over from the beginning without losing a beat. Good Luck!

Pattern

a Double Slide Step: sideways (R and L), forward, backward

b Double Touch Step: sideways (R and L), forward backward

c Cross Step: first tap R foot out to R side twice, (2 counts) then do the Cross Step on R side; tap L foot twice to L side (2 counts) then do Cross Step on L side

d Slide Step: to R and L side

Don't stop! Go back to the beginning while the beat goes on!

Recommended Practice Music:
slow: *You Make Me Feel Like Dancin'* (Leo Sayer)
fast: *Everybody Dance* (Chic)

BASIC DISCO STEPS

The hip moves are what help give disco dancing its unique style. If you don't get your hips going, then there's no "disco" in your dancing.

F.   HIP SHAKES

Start Position: feet diagonally apart (one foot front, the other back and knees slightly bent). Weight is even on both feet.

Description

Pick one hip (your favorite hip) and accent it out to one side (throw it sideways) on every beat. It should feel as though you're really moving your hips with feeling, yet fluidly. To get the feeling of accenting one hip, imagine that there's a little bell on only one side of your body next to your hip. The only time the bell rings is when your hip hits the bell button! Practice these "hip hits" to one side until it feels comfortable. Now try bending and straightening your knees on 4 or on 2 counts, all the while you're accenting one hip on *every* beat.

LEAN VARIATION

Keep accenting one hip sideways while you lean back on 4 counts so that most of your weight is on the back foot. Continue by leaning forward on 4 counts so that most of your weight is on the front foot. Practice leaning backward and forward (4 counts in each direction) without ever losing a beat in your hips!

Recommended Practice Music:
slow: *I Wish* (Stevie Wonder)
fast: *Boogie Oogie Oogie* (Taste of Honey)

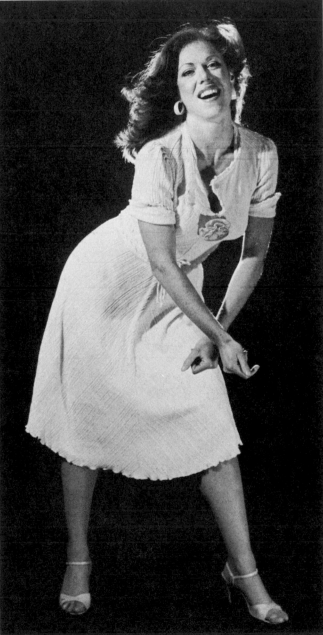

BASIC DISCO STEPS

Style

While the hips are shaking on every beat, your arms are not hanging down at your sides; they're constantly busy!

Arms

1 *The Roll:* roll arms up and down with your hands formed into fists

2 *The Fever:* raise one arm high every *other time* the hip accents to the side

3 Beckon your partner

4 Rebuff your partner

5 *The Pump:* pump your arms up and down while the hips move side to side

6 Make up your own arm combinations

BASIC DISCO STEPS

Remember the old Charleston heel—toe side to side step? This one isn't so different; all that's changed is the style. Rather than danced so energetically, this one is done subtly, giving the step a sexier look.

G.   FOOT SWIVELS

Start Position: feet about shoulder width apart with your weight even on both feet

Counts	Description
1	Twist both *heels* toward the R (to do this you'll need to put a little more weight toward the balls of your feet.
2	Twist your *toes* to the R (you'll be putting more weight on the heels)
3	Repeat count 1
4	Lift your L foot close to the R leg

Put L foot down then reverse the Foot Swivels to the L:

5	Twist both heels toward the L
6	Face toes L
7	Twist heels L
8	Lift the R foot close to the L leg

Continue the swivels from R to L non-stop.

4	1	2	3	4
4	heels	toes	heels	lift

Style

The feeling is a bit bouncy; your knees bounce down slightly on each count, and your arms swing forward and backward in a natural way. Your upper body doesn't lean or twist; keep it kind of quiet and let your feet, knees, hips, and arms do the moving. To exaggerate the "look," alternate pumping your arms up and down in front of you as if you were raising a large theater curtain, or as if you were milking a cow.

49

BASIC DISCO STEPS

DANCE #4: THE BODY LANGUAGE

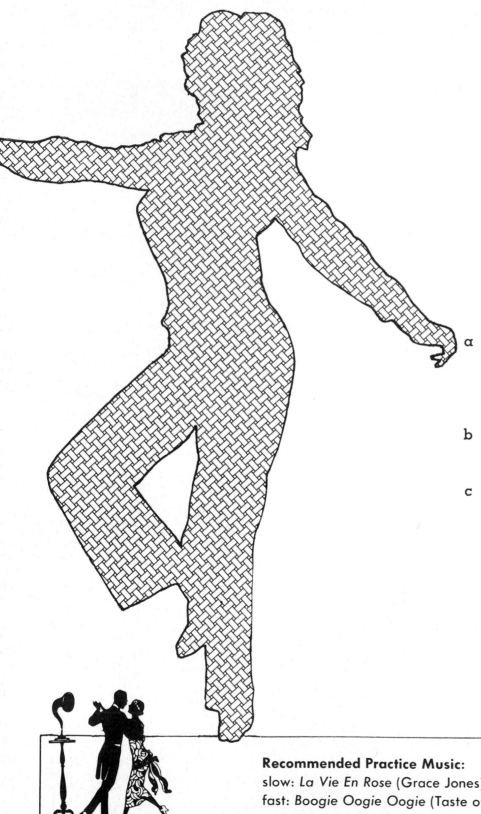

The real idea behind this dance is to communicate with your hands. In the hip shakes, the "language" is spoken with the arms and hands, while the hips keep the beat. The Foot Swivels and the Slide Step are used as a break. Without actually touching your partner, make up some way of "conversing" using your hands, (without losing a beat in the hips). This is a coordination feat in itself!

Pattern

a Hip Shakes: lean back on 4 counts, and forward for 4 counts. Repeat, and add arm-hand moves.

b Foot Swivels: to the R and L sides. Repeat.

c Slide Step: side to side, then forward, and backward. Immediately return to the Hip Shakes (Keep smiling).

Later try to mix and match these steps into your own pattern, or dance each step as many times as you like before moving on to the next step.

Recommended Practice Music:
slow: *La Vie En Rose* (Grace Jones)
fast: *Boogie Oogie Oogie* (Taste of Honey)

Here's one of the easiest of the hip moves that is practically germane to disco dancing. Your feet don't move on the first 3 counts; all the action is in your hips, so let them loose and keep them liquid smooth.

H.   THE SWAY

Start Position: Feet at least shoulder width apart, knees bent, weight even on both feet

Counts	Description
1	Push R hip out to R side and put weight on R foot (keeping knees bent)
2	Reverse to L: push L hip out and rock weight to L
3	Repeat count 1
4	Lift L leg and bring it close to the R one
	Reverse: set L foot down and...
5	Put weight on L foot and push L hip out to side
6	Put weight on R and push R hip to side
7	Repeat count 5
8	Lift R leg close to L one

Style

Feel the hips getting loose and sexy as they sway. Let your arms swing from side to side either opposite from or along with the hips.

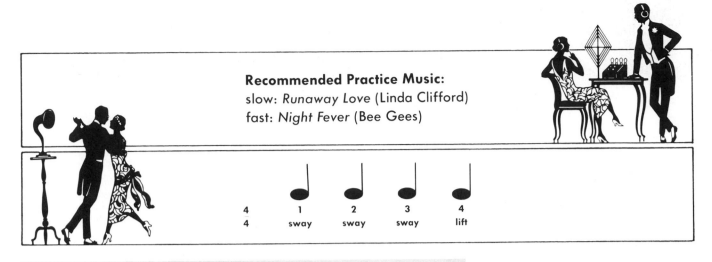

Recommended Practice Music:
slow: *Runaway Love* (Linda Clifford)
fast: *Night Fever* (Bee Gees)

4	1	2	3	4
4	sway	sway	sway	lift

BASIC DISCO STEPS

THE SWAY: **VARIATION**

FORWARD/BACKWARD VARIATION:

Start Position: R forward, L backward: feet comfortably apart, knees bent

Counts	Description
1	Push pelvis forward and transfer weight to R foot (knees still bent)
2	Transfer weight to L foot and stick out your buttocks
3	Repeat count 1
4	Lift L foot close to R one
5	Step L foot forward, put weight on it, and push pelvis forward
6	Push hips backward (stick out your bottom in back)
7	Repeat count 5 (push pelvis forward)
8	Lift R foot close to L one
1	Step R foot in back, put weight on R foot and push buttocks out in back
2	Push pelvis forward (weight on L foot)
3	Push hips backward (weight on R)
4	Lift L leg next to R
5	Set L foot down in back, put weight on it and release buttocks backward

6 Push pelvis forward (weight on R foot)

7 Push hips backward (weight on L)

8 Lift R foot and start all over from the beginning.

Style

The idea is to sway your hips forward and backward keeping your upper body and feet quiet. Let your arms swing naturally at your sides. You can exaggerate the hip moves by emphasizing the pelvic push forward and hips backward. Let your weight rock from one foot to the other. Be bold in the hips!

Here's the sexiest semicircle you'll ever draw. This is another hip move that gives disco its special style. Be prepared to let your hips undulate belly-dance style.

I. HIP SWIRLS (or 4 corners)

Start Position: Feet a little more than shoulder width apart and knees bent slightly. Weight is on the L foot.

Start: Draw a semicircle with your hips moving backwards from L to R. To do this you'll be sticking out your bottom and swinging your hips around back while you're transferring your weight from the L to R foot. Then swing hips around back again from R to L. Keep your hips swirling in a semicircle with the accent backward. You're changing weight from L, to both feet, to R foot as your hips swirl around.

Arms: Let arms swing across your body (one in front, the other in back), or open arms sideways while your hips swirl.

Style

If your knees are too stiff you won't get much hip action. Keep the knees comfortably bent and you'll be able to increase the size of your fluid semicircle.

LIFT VARIATION:

Lift your L foot on the 2nd count right after you semicircle your hips around to the R side. Set the foot down then swing hips around to the L (keep both feet on the floor). Every time your hips swing around to the R, lift the L foot, knee raised.

This quick step will get your feet hoppin'! You'll be taking tiny steps in place. If your toes are straight ahead you're dong the Roach step. If you turn the toes in (knock-kneed style) you're doing the Pidgeon. Notice that the accent is on the taps.

J.   THE ROACH (PIGEON) STEP

Start Position: Feet shoulder width apart

Counts	Description
and	Step on L (in place)
1	Tap the R (in place)
and	Step on R
2	Tap the L
and	Step on L
3	Tap the R
4	Kick the R (small, swift kick)
and	Step on R
5	Tap the L
and	Step on L
6	Tap the R
and	Step on R
7	Tap the L
8	Kick the L

Style

You're barely moving your feet; mostly you're tossing your weight from one foot to the other, accenting the tap rather than the step. Try the Pidgeon style

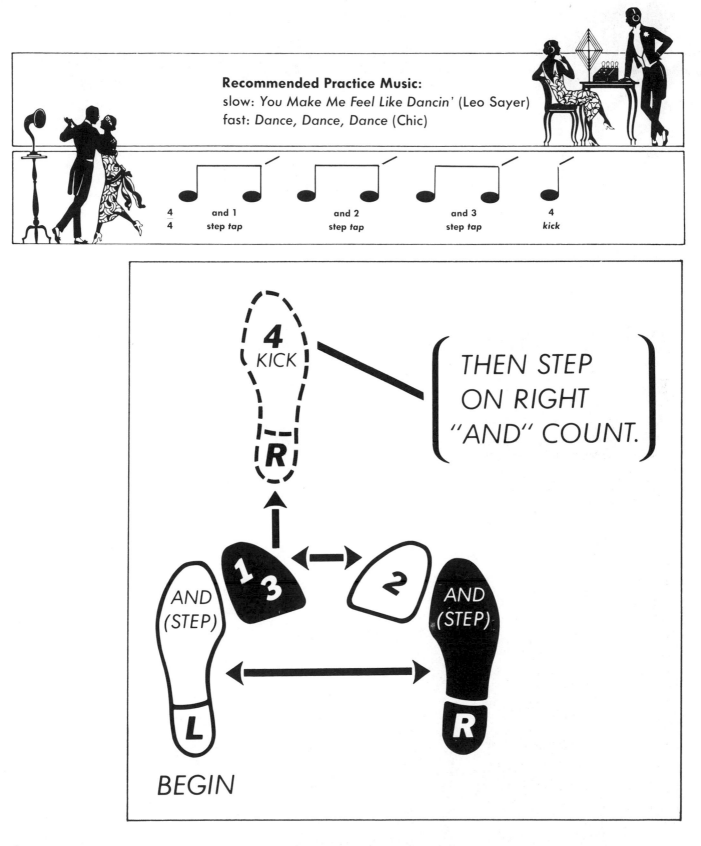

Recommended Practice Music:
slow: *You Make Me Feel Like Dancin'* (Leo Sayer)
fast: *Dance, Dance, Dance* (Chic)

4/4   and 1 *step tap*   and 2 *step tap*   and 3 *step tap*   4 *kick*

4 KICK R

THEN STEP ON RIGHT "AND" COUNT.

AND (STEP)

1 3

2

AND (STEP)

L

R

BEGIN

(toes turned in) and you'll get your hips swinging, naturally. One popular arm style is to bend the elbows up and out to the sides as if they were wings; or you could swing one arm straight out to the side while the other stays bent up like a wing ("half wing" it). Then wing it!

BASIC DISCO STEPS

DANCE #5: THE SWAY AND SWIRL

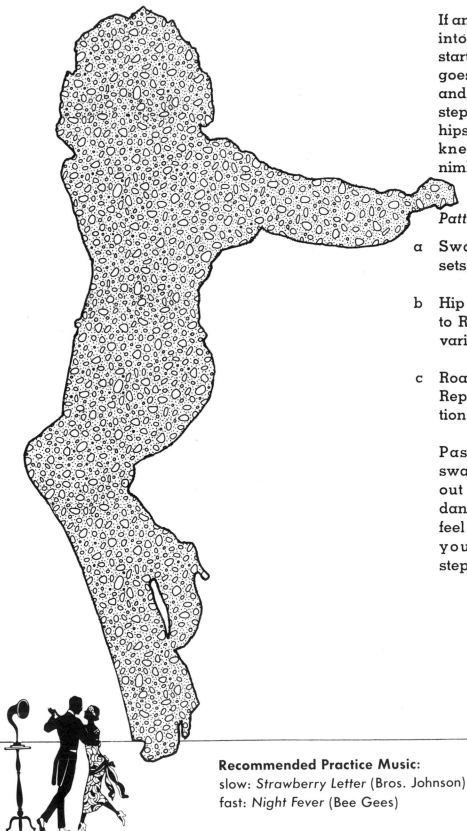

If any dance can call your hips into action, this one can! It starts with a smooth hip Sway, goes into a faster hip Swirl, and ends with a quick Pidgeon step. Think style: keep your hips fluid and animated, your knees loose, and your feet nimble. Enjoy yourself!

Pattern

a   Sway: forward/backward (2 sets) side to side (2 sets)

b   Hip Swirls: 4 Swirls (semicircle to R, L, R, L). Repeat using lift variation.

c   Roach Step on R & L sides. Repeat using Pidgeon variation.

Pass go, and immediately sway from the beginning without breaking the cycle. The dance stops when you start to feel hungry. Try a pattern all your own based on these steps.

Recommended Practice Music:
slow: *Strawberry Letter* (Bros. Johnson)
fast: *Night Fever* (Bee Gees)

BASIC DISCO STEPS

Instead of the hips moving from side to side, or forward to back, in the Scrunch they move from center to back with the accent on the back part. To put it more succinctly, you'll be sticking out your bottom on every beat, and doing it with feeling!

K. SCRUNCH HIPS

Starting Position: Feet a little further than shoulder width apart, knees bent.

Counts	Description
1	Put most of your weight onto one foot and stick out your buttocks by releasing your pelvis backward (look as though you're about to take a seat).
and	Return hips to center (normal) position, but keep your weight on the same foot and keep both knees bent
2	Repeat count 1
and	Return hips center and immediately transfer weight onto other foot
3	Repeat count 1 (with weight on other foot)
and	Return hips to center
4	Repeat count 3
and	Return hips center and transfer weight over to other foot.

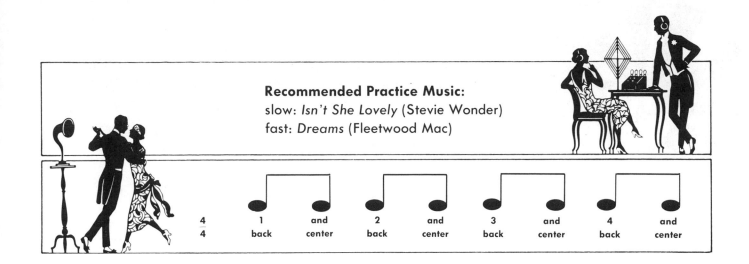

$\frac{4}{4}$

1	and	2	and	3	and	4	and
back	center	back	center	back	center	back	center

Style

The accent in your hips happens each time you throw them backward. Rather than jerking them backward, keep the movement from back to center to back, etc. very smooth.

If you feel ridiculous practicing this "move," it's because we don't routinely position our hips this way in normal life. On the disco floor though, the hips are supreme, so here's your chance to break them loose! Practice the scrunch continuously while you change your weight from one foot to the other on the odd numbered counts.

63

BASIC DISCO STEPS

Here's a favorite, highly stylized shuffle step popularized by Jackie Gleason and later reintroduced by various disco singing groups as part of their live acts. The step happens quickly, so keep your feet nimble and away they'll go!

L. JACKSON 5 (JACKIE GLEASON) *SHUFFLE*

THIS SHUFFLE IS ILLUSTRATED OVERLEAF

Starting Position: Feet about shoulder width apart

Counts	Description
1	Shuffle R foot (see glossary of terms)
2	Shuffle L
and	Kick R forward (small kick out)
3	Pull R foot in, heel across the L knee. If your R knee stays back, the position will imitate Jackie Gleason's "and away we go" move.
and	Repeat previous "and" count (kick R forward again)
4	Set R foot down
	Immediately repeat on L side:
5	Shuffle L foot back
6	Shuffle R foot back
and	Kick L forward slightly
7	Pull L in and across R knee (L knee back)
and	Repeat previous "and" count
8	Set L foot down

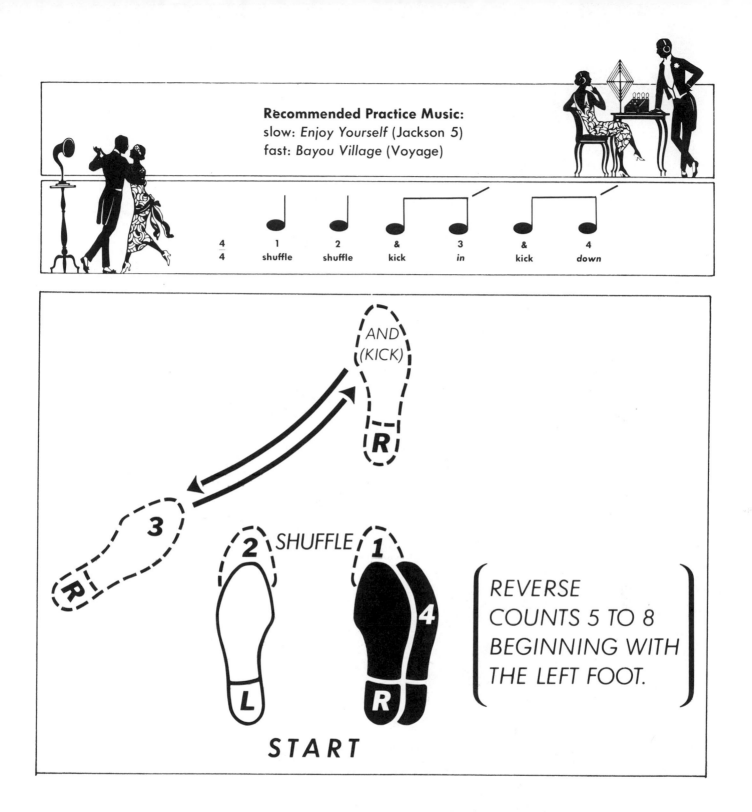

Recommended Practice Music:
slow: *Enjoy Yourself* (Jackson 5)
fast: *Bayou Village* (Voyage)

$\frac{4}{4}$

1	2	&	3	&	4
shuffle	shuffle	kick	in	kick	down

AND
(KICK)

R

3

SHUFFLE

2   1

R

L   4

R

REVERSE
COUNTS 5 TO 8
BEGINNING WITH
THE LEFT FOOT.

START

Style

This entire step is done a lot faster than it may appear from reading the directions, so begin by practicing it slowly non-stop until it feels smooth, then put on the music and pick up the pace. Keep your footwork small, and

Starting Position: Feet about shoulder width apart

Counts	Description
1	Shuffle R foot (see glossary of terms)
2	Shuffle L
and	Kick R forward (small kick out)
3	Pull R foot in, heel across the L knee. If your R knee stays back, the position will imitate Jackie Gleason's "and away we go" move.
and	Repeat previous "and" count (kick R forward again)
4	Set R foot down
	Immediately repeat on L side:
5	Shuffle L foot back
6	Shuffle R foot back
and	Kick L forward slightly
7	Pull L in and across R knee (L knee back)
and	Repeat previous "and" count
8	Set L foot down

your knees loose. The feeling is bouncy, especially on the shuffles.

Once this step feels comfortable, you can try traveling from side to side with it. When you're doing the two shuffle steps (counts 1 & 2) travel to one side (any side), and reverse direction on counts 5 & 6. Now put some exaggerated style into the step and have fun with it!

There's nothing like a turn to add flash and interest to a dance. Most people shy away from turns because they look difficult or disorienting. Well, fear no more; see for yourself what a cinch they are when they're broken down for you!

M.   HALF TURNS

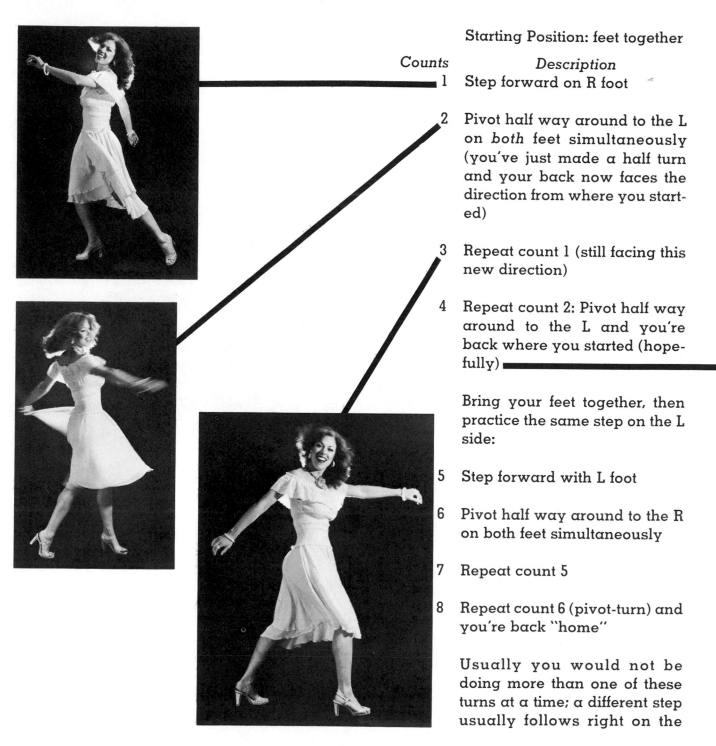

Starting Position: feet together

Counts	Description
1	Step forward on R foot
2	Pivot half way around to the L on *both* feet simultaneously (you've just made a half turn and your back now faces the direction from where you started)
3	Repeat count 1 (still facing this new direction)
4	Repeat count 2: Pivot half way around to the L and you're back where you started (hopefully)

Bring your feet together, then practice the same step on the L side:

5	Step forward with L foot
6	Pivot half way around to the R on both feet simultaneously
7	Repeat count 5
8	Repeat count 6 (pivot-turn) and you're back "home"

Usually you would not be doing more than one of these turns at a time; a different step usually follows right on the

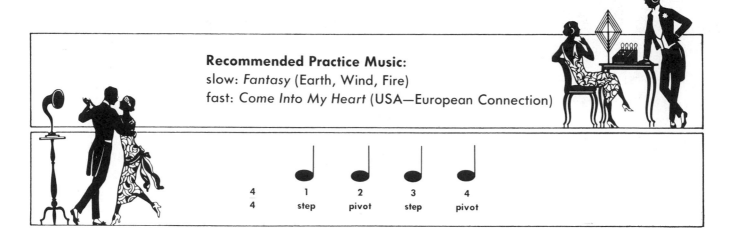

$\frac{4}{4}$ ♩ **1** step ♩ **2** pivot ♩ **3** step ♩ **4** pivot

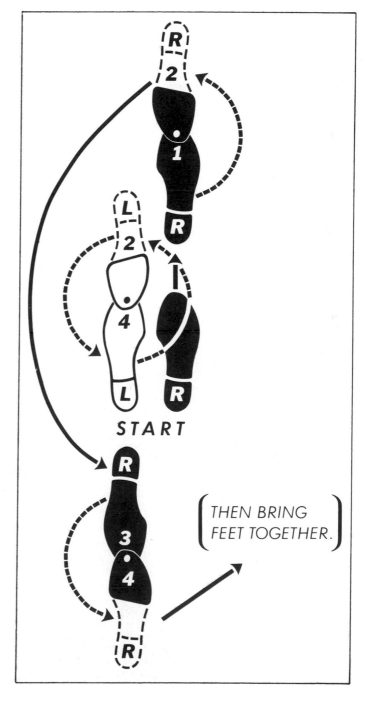

heels of this turn. If you wanted to try a chain of half turns, you'd need to adjust the foot pattern a bit: on count 4, pivot then immediately tap your L foot next to your R. Continue the turn on the L side, then on count 8 pivot-turn and immediately tap your R foot next to the L one.

THEN BRING FEET TOGETHER.

DANCE #6: THE SHUFFLE

To do the Shuffle with style, you need to think "funky." Let your body exaggerate the steps: really stick out your bottom in the Scrunch, keep the Shuffle Step loose and bouncy, and take big steps on the Half-Turn. Here's your chance to camp it up, so roll up your sleeves, get down, and put some soul into it!

Pattern

a   Scrunch Hips: 2 times with weight on R foot; 2 times with weight on L. Repeat R and L.

b   One Half-Turn (R side)

c   Jackson 5 (Jackie Gleason) Shuffle: R side (counts 1-4); L side (counts 5-8); R side again (counts 1-4)

d   One Half-Turn (L side)

e   Jackson 5 (Jackie Gleason) Shuffle: L side (counts 5-8); R side (counts 1-4); L side again (counts 5-8)

Immediately return to a Scrunch Hips and keep the dance in constant motion.

Recommended Practice Music:
slow: *Enjoy Yourself* (Jackson 5)
fast: *Bayou Village* (Voyage)

DANCE #7:   THE CITY SWIRL

Combine the Hip Swirls with the Foot Swivels and the Roach (Pidgeon) Step, and you have a tight little dance called the City Swirl. This one takes up hardly any room on the dance floor, but that doesn't mean you're not moving! Put some style into the steps, animate those swirling hips, and there'll be plenty of action in this dance!

Pattern

a   Hip Swirls: 4 swirls (semicircle to R,L,R,L). Repeat, using left variation.

b   Foot Swivels: to R and L. Repeat.

c   Roach Step. Repeat using Pidgeon variation.

Don't stop and think about what you've just done; return to the Hip Swirls immediately, lest you miss a beat!

Recommended Practice Music:
slow: *Enjoy Yourself* (Jackson 5)
fast: *Chattanooga Choo Choo* (Tuxedo Junction)

BASIC DISCO STEPS

DANCE #8:   NIGHT FEVER

Now we're ready to add more variety and try a more complicated dance. You're familiar with all of these steps from the previous pages, all you need remember is to keep moving. Don't let the transitions from one step into another throw you. If you follow the pattern carefully, your feet will automatically move through these four steps with Travolta-like ease. Good Luck!

Pattern

a Double Slide Step: to R and L side. Repeat using turn variation.

b Hip Shakes (lean variation): use any arm style you like

c Foot Swivels: to L and R sides. Repeat L and R.

d Roach (Pidgeon) Step

After the last Roach kick with the L foot, start the whole dance all over again from the Double Slide Step beginning to the L side this time.

Recommended Practice Music:
slow: *Night Fever* (Bee Gees)
fast: *Whistle Bump* (Deodato)

DANCE #9: TURNING POINT

Here it is, a disco dance that gives you a little challenge and a lot of variety. From slides to steps to shakes to turns, all the steps melt into one another like a river that flows continuously without beginning or end. You should be familiar with these steps by now, so don't panic. Relax and enjoy the dance!

Pattern

a Double Slide Step: side to side; forward to back

b Hip Shakes: lean variation (2 sets)

c Single Slide Step

d Half Turn

e Single Slide Step

f Double Slide Step (turn variation)

Go back to a) (Double Slide Step) without stopping to think about what you've just done! After this pattern feels comfortable (and it will), try the whole sequence on the L side by starting all your steps with the L foot; and if you make it through this dance, you've earned a Ph. Disco!

Recommended Practice Music:
slow: *Fantasy* (Earth, Wind, Fire)
fast: *Come Into My Heart* (USA—European Connection)

BASIC DISCO STEPS

Add a lot of style to this simple step, and it will look much more complicated than it really is. Accent counts 1 and 3 (the stepping counts) by exaggerating the knee bends.

N. THE BOUNCE STEP

Start Position: Feet together

Counts	Description
1	Step R to side and bend R knee. Dip over to the R side as if you were picking up a suitcase.
and	Stay there and bounce both knees down.
2	Slide L next to R (bend knees)
and	Bounce both knees down again with weight on both feet
3	Step L to side, and bend L knee (dip L)
and	Bounce both knees down
4	Slide R next to the L and bend knees
and	Bounce both knees down again with weight on both feet

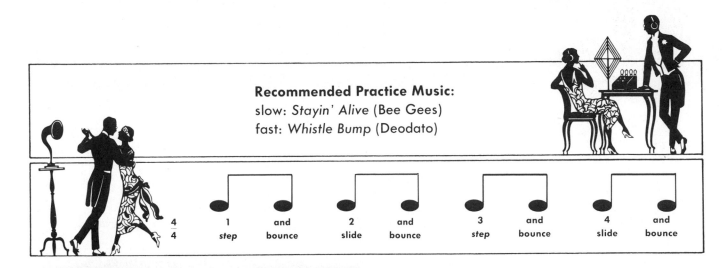

$\frac{4}{4}$

1	and	2	and	3	and	4	and
step	bounce	slide	bounce	step	bounce	slide	bounce

Style

When you take the first step on count 1, really bend that knee so you sink into the step. (Let your R hip push out to the side).

Arms: Stretch one arm to the side (the same arm as the stepping foot), and bend the other arm up at the elbow. Switch arm positions when stepping to the other side.

Shoulders: If you want to get fancy with this, shimmy your shoulders back and forth on each beat as if they were on a vibrator.

BASIC DISCO STEPS

THE BOUNCE STEP: **VARIATION**

FORWARD/BACKWARD
VARIATION:

Counts	Description
1	Step R diagonally forward and bend both knees low. (Lean your upper body forward.)
and	Bounce knees down.
2	Slide L next to R and bend knees (Straighten upper body)
and	Bounce both knees again, weight on both feet
3	Step L diagonally backward and bend knees. Lean backward a bit and put extra weight on the back foot (L)
and	Bounce knees down a bit
4	Slide R next to L (Straighten body)
and	Bounce knees down together, weight on both feet

To extend the forward/backward variation, on count 3 step the L foot forward again. Then repeat counts 1–4, stepping *backward* on counts 1 and 3.

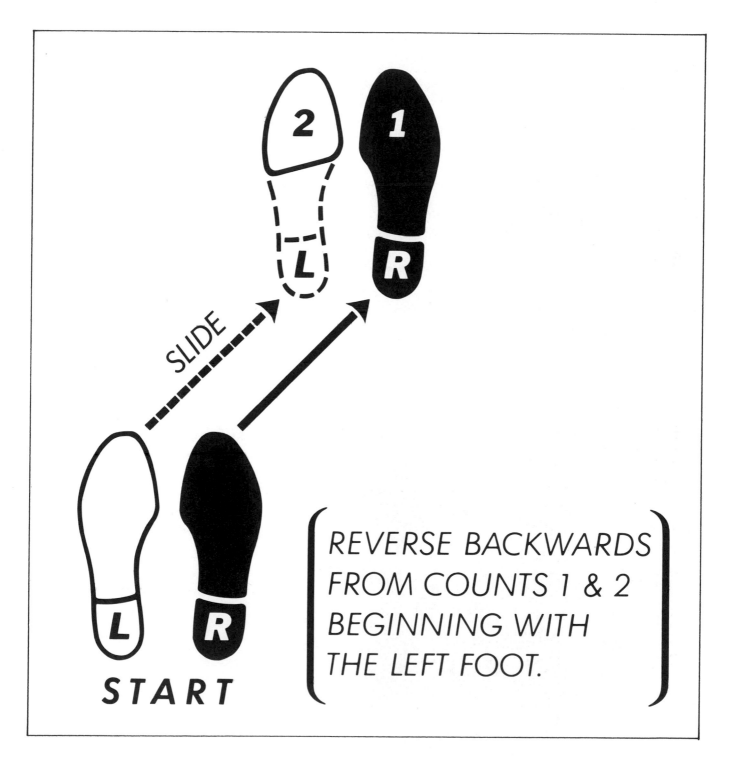

SLIDE

REVERSE BACKWARDS FROM COUNTS 1 & 2 BEGINNING WITH THE LEFT FOOT.

START

If you stand sideways to a partner, this hip movement could become the "Bump." Although the "Bump" may be passé by now, this hip movement on which it was based, still lives on the disco floor. You can forget your feet, they don't move at all. Only your hips initiate the action by moving in a modified "Z" pattern with the accent on the 1st and 3rd counts.

O.   BREAKDOWN HIPS

Starting Position: Feet a little more than shoulder width apart, weight even on both feet.

Counts	Description
1	Pick your favorite hip, let's say the R hip, and throw it out *sharply* to the R side as you transfer your weight onto the R foot. Let your R arm swing a little behind the R hip. Knees are straight, but not stiff.
2	Bend knees slightly and swing the L hip out and transfer your weight to L foot. L arm swings behind L hip a bit.
3	Bend knees lower and repeat count 1
4	Repeat count 2 (knees are only slightly bent)

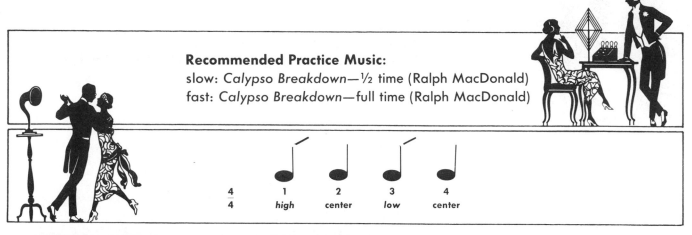

Recommended Practice Music:
slow: *Calypso Breakdown*—½ time (Ralph MacDonald)
fast: *Calypso Breakdown*—full time (Ralph MacDonald)

$\frac{4}{4}$

1	2	3	4
high	center	*low*	center

Style

Your hips are describing a zig-zag pattern that looks something like this:

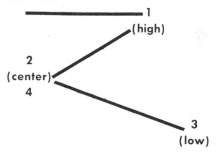

with the accent on the R hip high and low. Try the same pattern starting with the L hip.

DOUBLE VARIATION:

On counts 1 and 3 throw your hip out twice sharply. Since you have 2 hip throws to do in the same amount of time as you did one hip throw, you've got to make the hip moves smaller and faster!

This is the step that distinguishes line dances from all the other disco dances. Most of the more popular line dances incorporate this step at the end of the pattern or set sequence of steps. Usually this step is done only once to initiate a change in direction, then the dance starts all over facing the new direction (a ¼ turn to the left).

P. THE LINE TURN

Start: Feet together

Counts	Description
1	Tap R forward and swing arms naturally (L arm forward, R arm backward)
2	Tap R backward and swing arms in reverse
3	Tap R sideways and open arms to sides
4	Kick R foot across your body (in front) and make a ¼ turn to the L by pivoting on the ball of the L foot

You're facing a new direction and the line dance will start all over from the beginning.

Style

Let your arms swing in a natural, comfortable way on the taps. The knees are loose, not stiff.

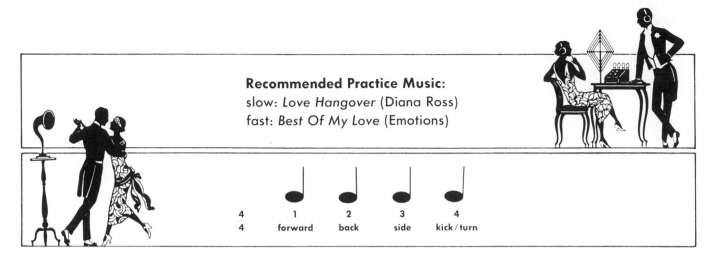
$\frac{4}{4}$	1	2	3	4
	forward	back	side	kick/turn

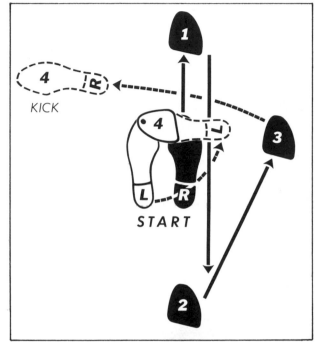

THE DOUBLE TAP (8-COUNT) VARIATION:

Counts	Description
1	Tap R forward
2	Repeat
3	Tap R backward
4	Repeat Count 3
5	Tap R forward
6	Tap R backward
7	Tap R sideways
8	Kick R across body and pivot ¼ turn to L on L foot

THE 4-COUNT VARIATION:

1	Tap R forward
2	Tap R sideways and simultaneously pivot ¼ to the L on the L foot
3	Tap R forward (facing new direction)
4	Tap R backward

DANCE #10:   THE ROCKING CHAIR

This is the most basic of all the line dances. Master this one, then go on to the more complicated line dances in Chapter III. The Bounce Step, the Breakdown Hips, and the Line Dance Turn (4 count variation) all combine into a smooth non-stop routine that faces 4 different directions (a ¼ turn changes the direction). Keep your knees loose, your hips very active, and your sense of direction clear!

Pattern

a   Bounce Step: forward, backward, side to side

b   Breakdown Hips: one set

c   Line Turn: the basic turn (or the 4 count variation)

After you've completed the line turn and find yourself facing a different wall (a ¼ turn to the L), start the pattern all over again from this new direction. You'll be repeating the pattern 3 more times before you wind up right back where you started from. Repeat the dance for as long as you like, or until you're dizzy.

Recommended Practice Music:
slow: *Strawberry Letter* (Bros. Johnson)
fast: *Whistle Bump* (Deodato)

DANCE #11: YOUR OWN COMBINATION (Free Style)

Well my terpsichorean friends, by now you're looking pretty good! You've got 16 basic disco steps down pat, and you can do 10 dances with the greatest of ease based on combinations of these 16 steps. Right? You should know that one exciting aspect of disco dancing is the total freedom you have to improvise and even to create your own dances from the alphabet of basic steps and variations. Play with all of the steps awhile, then try to combine them into your own inimitable pattern (or non-pattern) without stopping between transitions. You'll discover that certain steps blend better because the transitions from one to the other feel smoother. You may decide to abandon all dance patterns and just let the music move you through those steps you enjoy the most. After you've gained some experience with the music and steps, you'll begin to "sense" the music suggesting certain dances to you. Once your feet learn the alphabet of disco steps, combine them together in whatever way strikes your fancy, then go out there with your new dancin' feet and work up a storm!

The following pages contain a variety of additional disco moves and positions without offering a description of how to execute actual "steps." Now it's *your* turn to take some of these positions and make up your own step(s) for each, or to incorporate a few of these positions into your dancing. Once you familiarize yourself with the basics, you can become your own disco dance choreographer. Just let your creative juices flow!

BASIC DISCO STEPS

CHAPTER THREE

LINE DANCES

If you've ever fantasized about being in a real live chorus line, here's your big chance. *Everyone* loves line dances, the Busby Berkeley routines of the disco generation. A whole room full of dancers line up in rows all facing the same direction doing the same set pattern of steps, kicks, and turns, at the same time in the same style. The effect is stunning! Dancers share a feeling of comraderie and spiritual oneness as they all do the same high-energy routine. To an innocent bystander, the scene looks like a massive wave of frenzied lemmings headed out to sea. Take me to your leader! But in this kind of dancing there are no leaders, no followers, and no partners; everyone simply *knows* the routine (or learns it along the sidelines). All it takes is a small band of line "hustlers" to start in one corner of the floor, and like wildfire, everyone breaks into chorus line disco fever.

The routines of most (though not *all*) line dances begin by taking three walking steps backward, starting on the right foot; and end by making a one quarter turn to the left on the L foot. Then the routine starts all over facing the new (one quarter way around) direction.

There's no stopping between the time you complete the set routine (making a quarter turn) and the time it starts again facing the new direction. The beat goes on, and so does a line dance. Eventually, you drop from exhaustion or the disco closes. Busby Berkeley would have been proud!

DANCE #12: THE L.A. HUSTLE (Bus Stop)

This is the line dance that launched a thousand others. It debuted in Summer '75 in a small disco in Los Angeles, and enjoyed instant popularity. It didn't become a national breakout until Spring '76 when it hit the East Coast under the name the "Bus Stop." Some of the steps were modified during the migration, and after a while enough spinoffs were created to make line dances a permanent part of everyone's disco dance repertoire.

Two of the steps in Chapter II, the Double Slide Step and the Line Turn, are incorporated into this dance. There are four main sections to the L.A. Hustle, and they blend in sequence, making one highly choreographed line dance.

Style

Think strut: Swing your arms, dip your shoulders, and bounce your knees.

A. BACKWARD-FORWARD "LINE WALK":

Counts	Description
1	Step backward on R
2	Step backward on L
3	Step back on R
4	Touch L foot next to R

Reverse forward:

5   Step forward on L

6   Step forward on R

7   Step forward on L

8   Touch R next to L

Repeat counts 1–8 then go directly to part B

B. DOUBLE SLIDE STEP (CROSS VARIATION)

8 counts to R and L side

Repeat

Start part C.

C. JUMP-CLICKS:

1   Little jump forward on both feet

2   Hold

3   Little jump backward on both feet

4   Hold

5   Repeat count 1

6   Repeat count 3

7   Click heels together

8   Repeat heel clicks

and move on to part D

Recommended Practice Music:
slow: *The Hustle* (Van McCoy)
fast: *Scotch Machine* (Voyage)

D. LINE TURN (DOUBLE TAP VARIATION)—See Step P, Chapter II

When you and fellow dancers complete the line turn and end up ¼ way around to your L, the whole dance starts all over from Section A, (facing this new direction). Essentially you'll be facing a new wall each time you begin the routine from "A." All together now....

DANCE #13: THE HOLLYWOOD LINE HUSTLE

This dance followed hot on the heels, so to speak, of the L.A. Hustle. It has always been one of the most popular line-dances, and I'm always receiving requests to teach it. Now you can have the routine for yourself. This one is considerably more complicated than the L.A. Hustle because it has more steps in each of the 4 sections, but it begins the same way (with the "Line Walk") and it ends with a kick-turn ¼ way around to the left. The middle section incorporates the Single Slide Step and Half Turn from Chapter II.

At first glance this routine may look impossible. Don't despair, first learn each section separately then put them together in sequence. You'll be amazed at how smoothly all the parts fit together. Surprise yourself!

A. BACKWARD-FORWARD LINE WALK:

Counts	Description
1	Step R backward
2	Step L backward
3	Step R backward
4	Touch L foot next to R
	Reverse forward:
5	Step L forward
6	Step R forward
7	Step L forward
8	Touch R foot next to L and go directly to section B

B. Single Slide Step:

1	Step R sideways
2	Slide L next to R
3	Step L sideways
4	Slide R next to
5	Step R in place
6	Step L in place
7	Step R in place
and	Touch L in place
8	Step R

C. HALF-TURN (SEE STEP M CHAPTER II):

1 Step L forward

2 Pivot ½ way around

3 Repeat count 1 (in new direction)

4 Repeat count 2 (return "home")

5 Step L in place

6 Step R in place

7 Touch L sideways

8 Touch L in place (next to R)

D. STEPS—¼ TURN (PAY CLOSE ATTENTION):

1 Touch L sideways

2 Touch L next to R

3 Step L forward slightly

4 Step R in place

5 Step L back slightly

6 Touch R next to L

7 Touch R sideways

8 Kick R across body and pivot ¼ way around to L on L foot...

and the dance begins all over again from Section A facing this new direction.

DANCE #14: THE LUST HUSTLE

How could I resist? I tried to choreograph a line dance that would challenge even the most sophisticated line "hustlers." The routine has 6 sections (A–F), and some of the steps are already described for you in Chapter II: The Double Slide Step, Cross Step, and Swivel. You already know the Line Walk from the two previous line dances in this chapter, so the whole routine shouldn't be all that difficult! Smile, you're on!

A. BACKWARD-FORWARD LINE WALK

B. DOUBLE SLIDE STEP (TURN VARIATION) TO R AND L SIDE
(see Step D, Ch. II)

C. CROSS STEP (MODIFIED):

Counts	Description
1	Step forward on R
2	Cross L over R (put weight on L)
3	Step R backward
4	Step L next to R

Counts 5-8: Repeat counts 1-4, except on the 8th count just *touch* L next to R.

Reverse Cross Step (counts 1-8) starting with L foot.

D. WALKS
Take 4 walking steps backward starting with your R foot

E. STOMPS:

1	Step R forward
2	Lift L knee next to R
3	Step L forward
4	Lift R knee next to L
5	Stomp (or stamp) R foot down in place
6	Hold
7	Repeat count 5
8	Repeat count 5

F. SWIVELS: (MODIFIED)
This is a bit tricky. Do 4 foot swivels, as in step G, Chapter II, (heels, toes, heels, toes), but instead of traveling sideways, do the swivels in place and make a ¼ turn to your L while your feet are swiveling around. Now you're facing ¼ to your L (a different wall) and you begin the whole routine from "A" without a resting stop between sections and without a breather after the "Swivel-turn." There's no mercy in this line hustle!

Recommended Practice Music:
slow: *Love Hangover* (Diana Ross)
fast: *Johnny, Johnny Please Come Home* (Claudja Barry)

CHAPTER FOUR

PARTNER DISCO DANCES

Opinions differ as to how the disco partner dances originated. Some say they were created in early 1975 by Latinos in Manhattan; others say they are a direct decendant of the Jitterbug and Swing. Clearly some of the foot patterns and turns are reminiscent of the Jitterbug, Lindy, Swing and Rhumba. Yet, some of the syncopated 6 count foot patterns and flowing turns do incorporate a Latin style and feeling. Whatever the origin, these dances have gained a permanent popularity on the disco floor.

Most partner hustles have a 6 count foot pattern done to disco music with 4-4 timing, making them syncopated dances. All of them involve fast, intricate, and imaginative turns. There is no set pattern or number of turns; originality and personal interpretation decide the turn routine that partners develop (often spontaneously). Being in a disco filled with partner "hustlers" is an hypnotic experience, like attending a whirling dervish ceremony where nonstop dancers eventually seem to dematerialize, leaving only their continuous swirl of colorful clothing.

Unlike the Jitterbug or Lindy, which have a jerky push-pull feeling, partner hustles take on a smooth, gliding, sophisticated style. The foot pattern and turns may vary, but there are some basic similarities.

All partner disco dances begin in ballroom "closed" position then break out into "open" position for the fancy turns. In "closed" position partners stand close together facing each other. His R hand is just above her L waist. His L hand and her R hand are clasped with arms extended slightly to the side just below shoulder height. Her L hand rests on his R shoulder. If you can recall how Fred and Ginger danced together in the old-time movies, you'll immediately be able to assume this position. In disco "open" position, you and your partner are facing each other clasping one or both hands… you're always touching.

Who's the leader? In ballroom dancing the man *always* leads, even if he can't. In disco, usually the guy leads. Yet, a dancing female is no longer obliged to follow in the two left footsteps of a non-dancing male. If she has skill and timing, then be practical and "hand" her the lead. If you're both fairly well matched in ability, you can alternate leadership. Try to lead with your body instead of your mouth. A smooth adjustment in an arm movement, a gentle but firm pressure from one hand, a twist in the torso, all signal a change in direction; and are best accomplished just *before* the beat. Partner hustles do not progress in a counter clockwise "line of direction" around the room. They're done in a small circle of space that partners carve out just for themselves.

A. FOOT PATTERNS (HIS AND HERS)

I recommend that you and your partner begin by practicing one of the foot patterns in place, then move around with it in a small area. Once the footwork feels comfortable, move on to the turns. Smile at each other occasionally, and enjoy it!

DANCE #15:   SIMPLE PARTNER HUSTLE

If you've never partner danced before, this is a great step to get you started; then you can later graduate to the more complicated partner hustles. Remember to start by practicing the footwork alone; then hold hands and dance together, add some turns, and engage in light conversation. You know you've got it when you can look your partner in the eyes, instead of at your feet. In this dance, accent the tap.

Starting Position: Feet together

Counts	*Description*
1	She: Tap R foot to side (slightly); He: Tap L to side
2	Beginning with whichever foot
3	you tapped in count 1 take 3
4	small walking steps. You may walk in any direction your fancy takes you.
5	She: Tap L foot to side; He: Tap R to side
6	Beginning with the foot you
7	just tapped in count 5, take 3
8	small walking steps in any direction.

Return to count 1 and keep on dancing. Notice that the foot you tap on count 1 will be different from the foot you tap on count 5 (i.e. if you tap the L on count 1, you'll be tapping the R on count 5). The walking steps are done smoothly, but with soul!

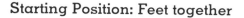

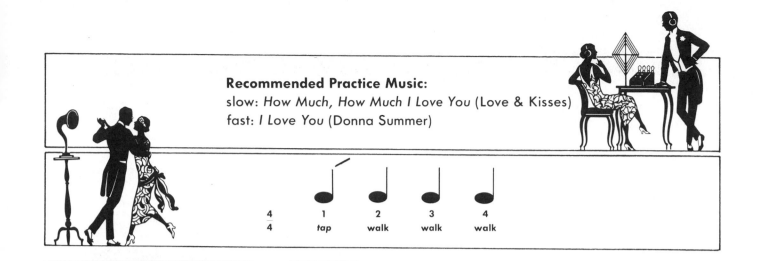

Recommended Practice Music:
slow: *How Much, How Much I Love You* (Love & Kisses)
fast: *I Love You* (Donna Summer)

4/4	1	2	3	4
	tap	walk	walk	walk

VARIATION
The taps are done sideways, but the 3 little walking steps may be taken in place; or you can move forward with them; you can "walk" backward; you can "walk" around in a circle; turn around yourself; or cross over (as in the case of the "cross-over turn" where you and your partner change places on the walks). Practice all of the above until they feel smooth, then hold hands and try all of the variations together.

DANCE #16: CONTINENTAL HUSTLE
(HER VERSION)

The basic footwork to this dance is very reminiscent of a lindy step popularized by our forefathers in the 1940's, only the Lindy started with a tap, and this dance begins with a step. If you ever danced a controlled Lindy, you'll adapt well to the Continental Hustle. After you and your partner feel comfortable with the basic footwork, hold hands ("open position"), or assume a ballroom ("closed") position and dance your respective versions together "Fred and Ginger" style. I've found that it's easier to learn this dance if you use 2-4 timing, giving every step one beat and accenting the 2nd and 4th counts.

Starting Position: Feet together, weight on L foot

Counts	Description
1	Step R foot slightly to R side
2	Tap L next to R
3	Step L to L side
4	Tap R next to L
5	Take two small walking steps
6	in any direction you like, starting with R foot (walk R; walk L)

Immediately return to count 1 and continually repeat without taking time out for tea.

Recommended Practice Music:
slow: *More Than A Woman* (Bee Gees)
fast: *Manhattan Skyline* (David Shire)

DANCE #16: CONTINENTAL HUSTLE
(HIS VERSION)

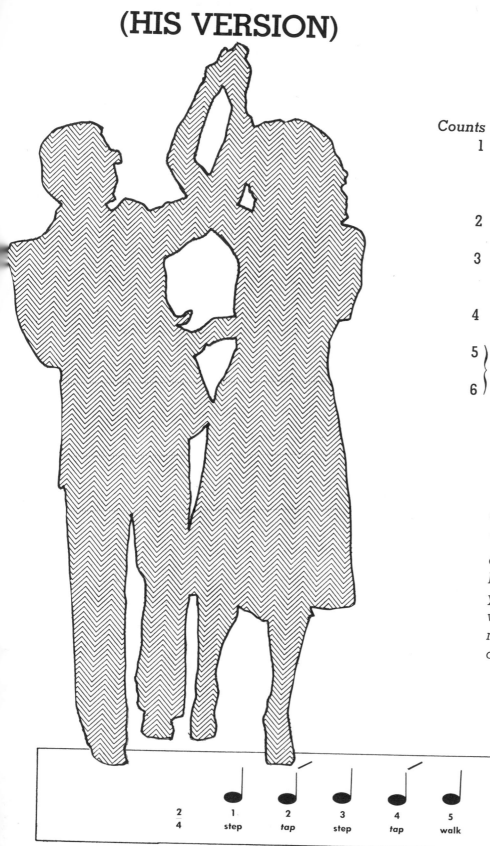

Starting Position: Feet together, weight on R foot

Counts	Description
1	Step L foot a bit to the L side and let your upper body lean slightly L
2	Tap R next to L
3	Step R foot slightly to R side and lean over a bit to the R
4	Tap L next to R
5 ⎫	Take two walking steps in any
6 ⎭	direction starting with L foot (walk L, walk R):

Then immediately return to count 1 and keep moving.

Style

Your steps are small and lively: a controlled bounce done with a hint of soul. On counts 1 and 3 you can step forward, backward, or initiate a turn. Practice moving in a variety of directions.

2/4	1 step	2 tap	3 step	4 tap	5 walk	6 walk

DANCE #17: LATIN-SWING HUSTLE

HIS VERSION

The Latin Hustle has often been referred to as *the* partner dance of the 70's. Actually, there are several variations of the Latin Hustle; the footwork differing from city to city, from disco to disco, and from instructor to student. Ultimately, the differences depend upon the amount of improvisation and imagination dancing partners incorporate into their steps and turns. In my travels I have observed that the Latin-Swing Hustle is the most popular of the Latin Hustle variations, even to the extent that attempts have been made to standardize the foot pattern. If you ever did the Lindy or the Swing in the 40's and 50's, you should do quite well with this foot pattern, which is really a combination of the double and the triple Swing steps.

It's easier to learn this dance by practicing it in 2-4 time, with the accents on the 2nd and 4th counts, so go to it!

Starting Position: Feet together, weight on R foot

Counts	Description
1	Tap L foot in place or slightly sideways
2	Step on L (in same place where you just tapped it)
3	Step R } 3 little "cha-cha-cha"
and	Step L } steps (or "step-ball
4	Step R } change" in tap language) may be taken in any direction, including turning around yourself. Keep them small and nimble.
5	Step L } two walking steps in
6	Step R } any direction you desire; or "step, step" in place.

NOW RETURN TO COUNT 1

Remember to practice the steps in place first, then move around with them when the footwork feels comfortable.

Note: Footcharts show the man moving forward and the woman moving backward. This is only one of the many directions partners can take with this step.

$\frac{2}{4}$	1	2	3	and	4	5	6
	tap	step,	cha-	cha-	cha,	walk	walk

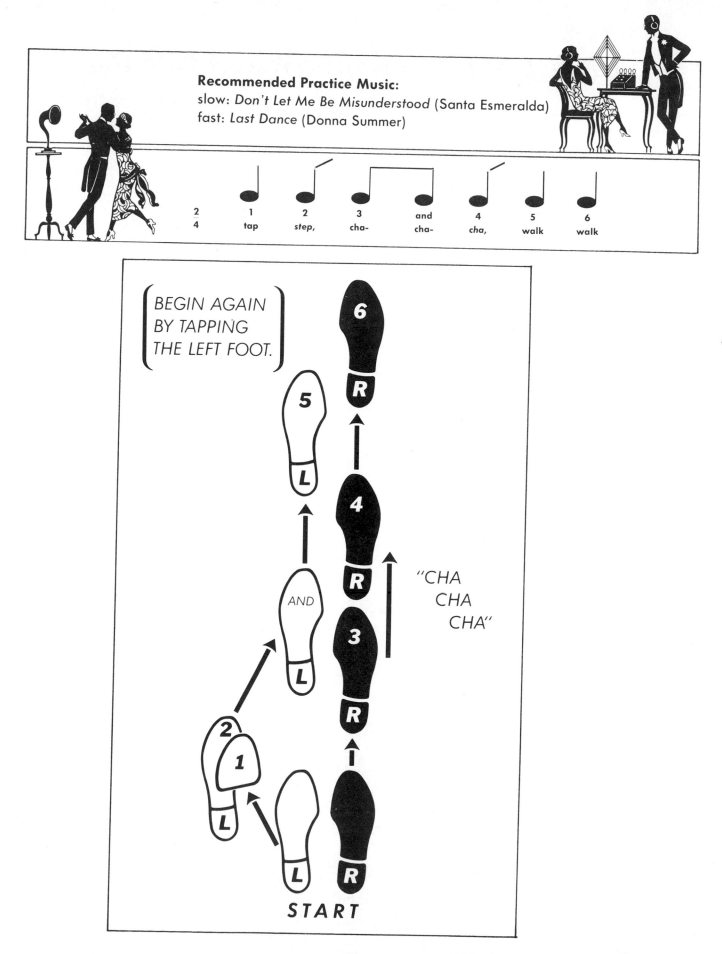

BEGIN AGAIN BY TAPPING THE LEFT FOOT.

"CHA CHA CHA"

START

DANCE #17: LATIN-SWING HUSTLE (HER VERSION)

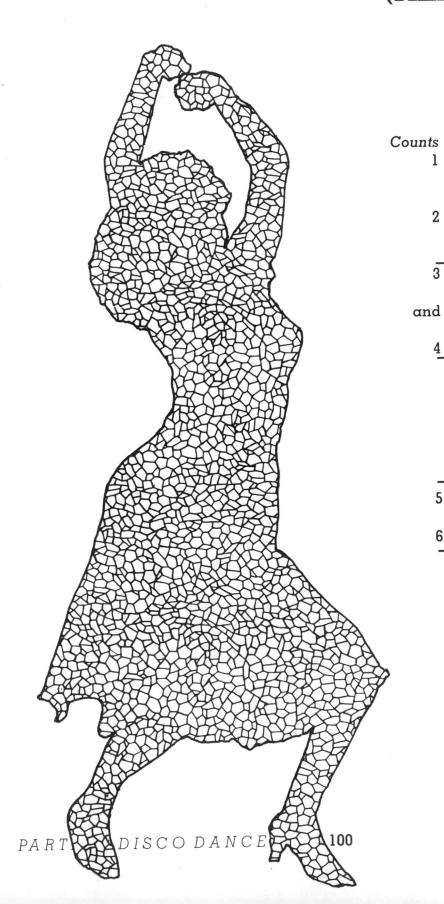

Ladies start with the R foot, and accent the 2nd and 4th counts

Starting Position: Feet together, weight on L

Counts	Description
1	Tap R foot in place or slightly sideways
2	Step on R (in same place where you just tapped it)

3 — Step L ⎫
and — Step R ⎬ These 3 little "cha-cha-cha" steps (or
4 — Step L ⎭ "step-ball-change") may be taken in place or in any direction (including turning around yourself). Keep them small and nimble.

5 — Step R ⎫
6 — Step L ⎬ two walking steps in any direction; you choose; or "step, step" in place.

NOW RETURN TO COUNT 1

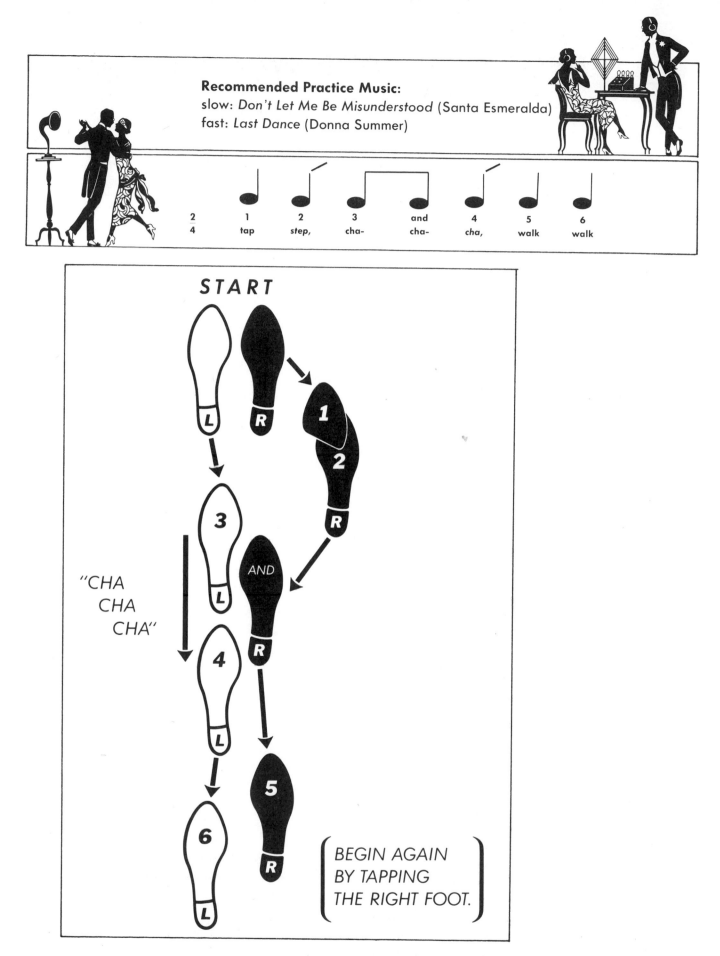

Recommended Practice Music:
slow: *Don't Let Me Be Misunderstood* (Santa Esmeralda)
fast: *Last Dance* (Donna Summer)

2/4

1	2	3	and	4	5	6
tap	step,	cha-	cha-	cha,	walk	walk

START

"CHA CHA CHA"

BEGIN AGAIN
BY TAPPING
THE RIGHT FOOT.

DANCE #18: LATIN HUSTLE VARIATION
(Cha Cha Cha variation)

I find that the footwork to this variation is by far the most challenging and the most beautiful. At first this step may seem too complicated but don't be discouraged! It does take practice and commitment, so expect to lose the step every so often at first. You only dance this step as a break between turns. It helps to say, "Tap, cha-cha-cha, walk, walk, walk" out loud until the routine is cemented in your head. True, you won't be a fascinating conversationalist, but you will learn the footwork faster. It's worth a try! The accent is on the tap...Good Luck!

HER VERSION

Starting Position: Feet together, weight on L

Counts		Description
1		Tap R in place (or to R side)

2	Step R	"quick-quick-quick"
and	Step L	or "cha-cha-cha" or
3	Step R	"step-ball-change" (whatever gives you the feeling of taking 3 little steps, alternating feet). You may take them in place or backward, or forward.

4	Step L	You can walk (travel)
5	Step R	on these 3 steps by
6	Step L	heading forward, backward, or by turning. These 3 steps cover a bit more distance than the 3 "steplets" you did in counts "2-and-3". Now begin again on your R foot with count 1.

Style:

Usually the tap is done in place. Practice dancing apart, together, and crossing over (changing places).

$\frac{3}{4}$

1	2	and	3	4	5	6
tap,	*cha-*	*cha-*	*cha,*	*walk*	*walk*	*walk*

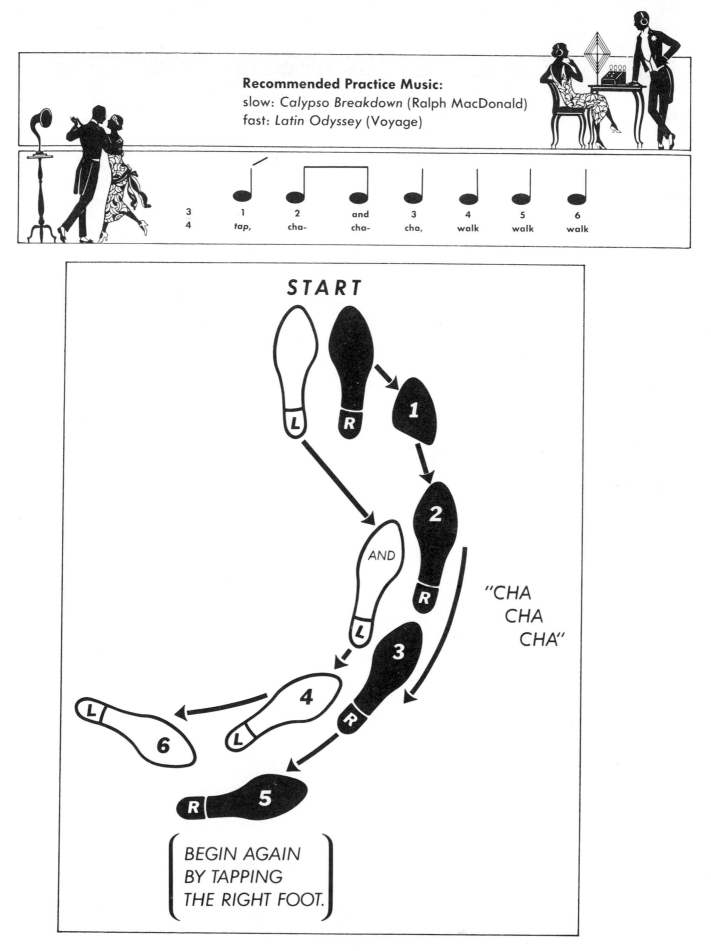

START

"CHA
CHA
CHA"

BEGIN AGAIN
BY TAPPING
THE RIGHT FOOT.

DANCE #18: LATIN HUSTLE VARIATION
(HIS VERSION)

Starting Position: Feet together, weight on R

Counts	Description
1	Tap (touch) L in place or slightly to L side

2	Step L	3 little steps ("cha-
and	Step R	cha-cha") taken in
3	Step L	place or in any direction, including turning around yourself

4	Step R	3 walking (traveling)
5	Step L	steps that cover a bit
6	Step R	more distance than the previous "cha-cha-cha" steps. Take these steps in any direction, depending on the routine you're doing with your partner. Then begin again with count 1 on your L foot.

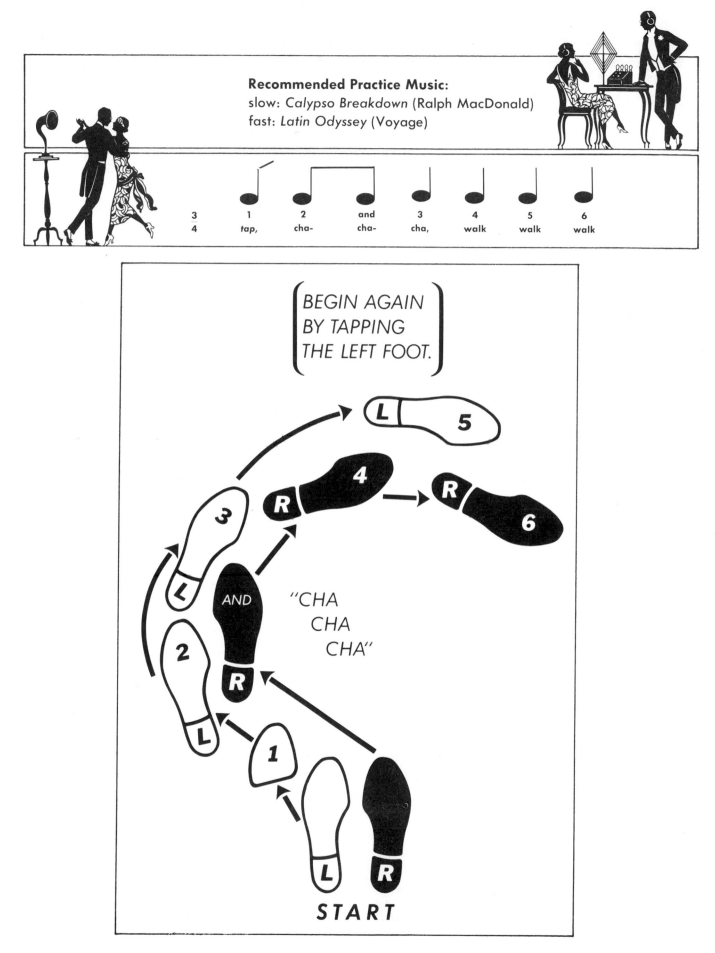

Recommended Practice Music:
slow: *Calypso Breakdown* (Ralph MacDonald)
fast: *Latin Odyssey* (Voyage)

$\frac{3}{4}$ | 1 tap, | 2 cha- | and cha- | 3 cha, | 4 walk | 5 walk | 6 walk

BEGIN AGAIN BY TAPPING THE LEFT FOOT.

"CHA CHA CHA"

START

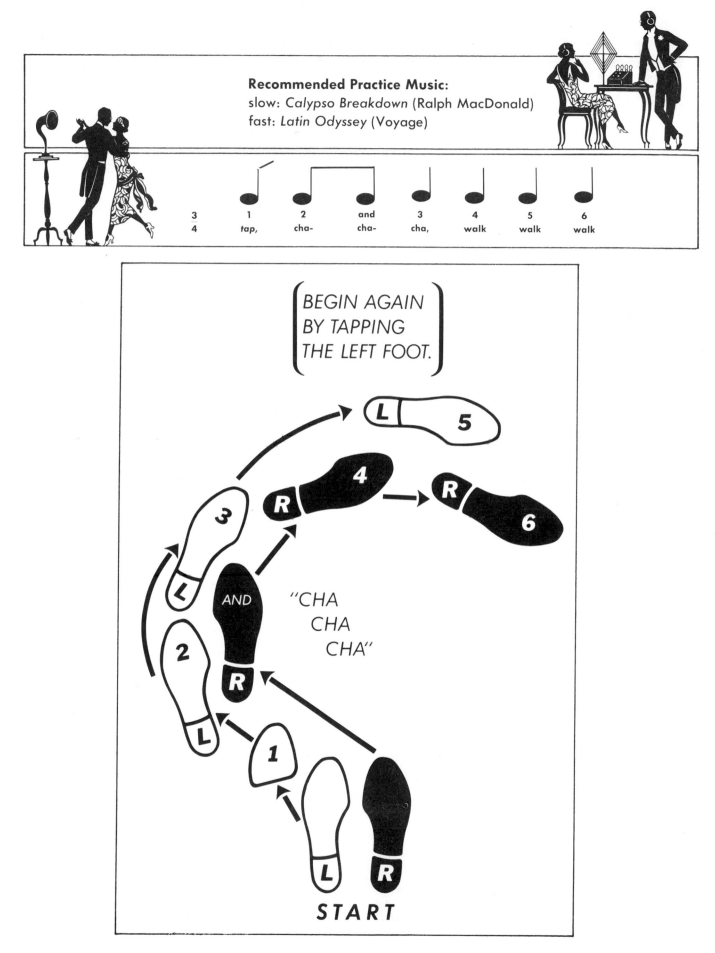

DANCE #19: LATIN HUSTLE (kick variation)

Thank the partner "hustlers" in Los Angeles and New York for popularizing this challenging foot pattern. It *is* an intricate step, so practice it slowly and frequently, repeating the counts over and over again in your sleep until the rhythm becomes imbedded in your mind.

Once you are able to count out the rhythm to your favorite records, try getting your feet wet. You'll do better if you keep your steps small and "tight" (close together). Practice the foot pattern in place first, then try to move slightly sideways, forward, or backward. Accent the tap and the kick.

His Version

Start: Feet together, weight on R

Counts	Description
1	Tap L foot (in place)
2	Step on L (slightly out to side, forward or back)
3	Step R (near L)
and	Step on L
4	Kick R foot (small, quick kick)
and	Step R (any direction)
5	Step L (any direction)
6	Step R (any direction)

Her Version

Counts	Description
1	Tap R (in place)
2	Step on R
3	Step L (near R)
and	Step on R
4	Kick L (small)
and	Step on L (any direction)
5	Step on R (any direction)
6	Step on L (any direction)

Repeat from count 1 and continue non-stop.

Recommended Practice Music:
slow: *Don't Let Me Be Misunderstood* (Santa Esmeralda)
fast: *Romeo and Juliet* (Alex Constandinos)

| 2/4 | 1 tap | 2 step | 3 step | and step | 4 kick | and step | 5 step | 6 step |

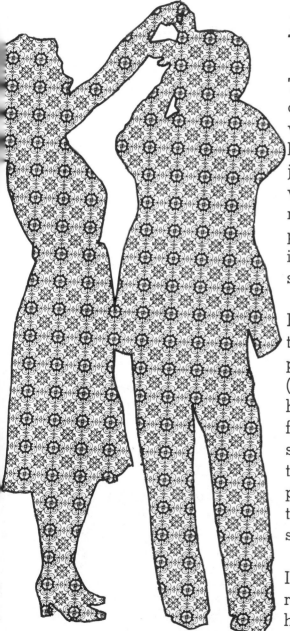

B.   BASIC PARTNER TURNS

Turns give flash, excitement, and beauty to partner disco dancing. You could do any of the foot patterns without turning (and they would still be challenging), but your dancing will lack excitement. Or you could do just the turns without a foot pattern, but your dancing will lack refinement and sophistication, and it will look more like a push-pull contest between you and your partner. It's the combination of foot pattern and interesting turns that make partner disco dances so spectacular.

Before you begin, there are a few tips about turning that you might find helpful. Turns usually begin with partners facing each other holding one or both "hands" (hers on top of his, if he's leading). Actually, partners hold *fingers* somewhat loosely allowing enough freedom for the fingers to turn, yet giving enough support to the hand of the turning partner. If your grip is too tight, gangrene sets in, or you break a wrist. Since partners are always holding one or both hands while turning, the wrists and arms need to be relaxed yet supportive: not too stiff, but not too flaccid.

In ballroom dancing the man initiates a turn usually by raising his L arm and guiding her under it with his R hand. In disco, it doesn't matter who initiates the turn

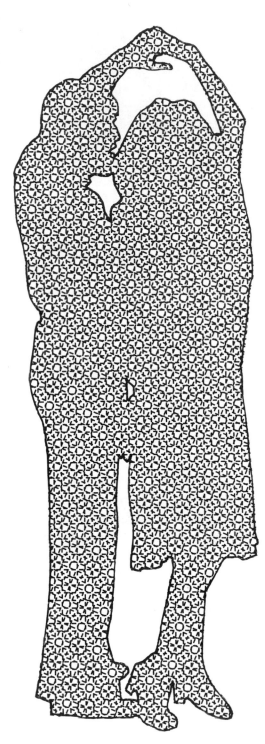

(whoever is leading), nor which arm she (or he) turns under. In fact, both partners develop proficiency in turning under either arm.

When following the instructions, keep in mind that there are only two directions in which you can turn: to the R and L; or to the outside (away from your other set of arms), and inside (toward your other set of arms). If you find yourself very tangled and crying for help, chances are you turned the wrong way!

In this chapter I've presented some of the more popular partner turns from simple to complex. Actually there are many more ways of turning, and as you familiarize yourself with the basic turns in this chapter, you and your partner will become creative enough to invent a few of your own.

Try repeating the same turn to one side, then repeat it by alternating sides. Alternate the same turn with your partner, and finally try stringing together several different turns.

The idea is to combine all the turns into any sequence you like so that, like the music, you're dancing and turning become continuous and smooth without any abrupt pauses. When you combine a few turns together you'll have to abandon your foot pattern. Then pick up the foot pattern again *between* sets of turns as a break from all that spinning. Have fun!

1. SIMPLE UNDERARM TURN

When in "closed position," he lifts his L arm nice and high and she passes under it, making a 360° turn (in disco, it doesn't really matter which way she turns).

When in "open" position, he can lift either arm for her to turn under. Of course, she can initiate the underarm turn just by lifting either arm and passing under it herself. Or, he can turn under either lifted arm, too. It's loose.

VARIATION—CONTINUOUS UNDERARM TURNS:

Keep one arm raised high while your partner turns under it several times quickly (more than twice). To accomplish this smoothly, the turning partner (let's say "she") abandons the foot pattern and spins around while describing a circular pattern on the dance floor. He also abandons the footwork and "walks" around her quickly while his raised "turning" arm supports and spins her. His arm aids her spinning by circling above but close to her head like a top. If his arm is too stiff, or his grip is too tight, he breaks her fingers. She is actually gripping two or three of his fingers (not his whole hand) while she spins.

2. UNDERARM CROSSOVER TURN

This one is almost the same as the simple underarm turn, only you're changing places at the same time the turn occurs. Face each other with a one-handed grip in open position. While she turns under his arm, both advance forward passing each other to one side (any side). When partners have actually changed places, they pivot around to face each other (and to face the new direction). Walk through this, then try the turn while doing a foot-pattern. Often this turn is done several times back and forth with either she, he, or both turning under while changing places. Don't go too far away from each other while changing places or turning.

3. PEEK-A-BOO TURN

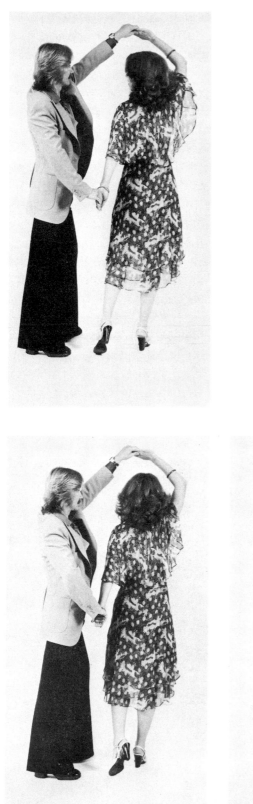

Here's a tricky little hand-holding half-turn. Partners face each other and hold hands (loosely). He lifts his L (or R) arm high for her to pass under. She turns half way under (to the *outside*) so that her back is to him with one set of hands clasped high over her head, and the other set of hands clasped at the back of her waist (her elbow bent). Partners can glance over one shoulder to get a "peek" at each other for re-assurance. Then she returns under the same arm from whence she came (to the *out-side*) and faces him. Notice that partners never drop hands.

Practice "walking" through this turn: she under his L arm, then she tries the same turn under his R arm. He does this turn, too (under her L and R arm). Finally try alternating: she under his L; he under her R; vice-versa, or any other combination you can come up with.

Once you can walk through this turn smoothly and contin-uously, alternating with each other and without getting tan-gled, then you know you're ready to combine it with a foot pattern. If you string several peek-a-boo turns together, then abandon the foot pattern and "walk" through the turns very quickly.

4. WAIST CROSS

Once you've done the Peek-a-boo turn, this one should be easy.

Partners face each other and hold hands. He lifts his L (or R) arm high for her to pass under. She turns under (to the *outside*), but this time she doesn't stop the turn half-way with her back to him (like in the Peek-a-boo turn). Instead, she continues the turn, ending up side by side (partners facing opposite directions) with one set of hands clasped at *his* belly button, and the other set of hands clasped at the back of *her* waist (her elbow is bent).

Now, if you got into this position, you should be able to get out of it, right? What goes around comes around: he raises the arm that's in front of his belly button, she turns under it to face him, and partners are back where they started.

Now it's *his* turn (literally) and he puts himself in her shoes, so to speak, to the R and L side. (When he does this turn, *his* arm is bent behind his waist and the other set of hands are clasped in front of *her* navel.) The idea is to do several of these waist-cross turns non-stop under the L & R arm, alternating with each other.

5. WRAP-UNWRAP TURN

In this turn each partner is wrapped by the other, unless there happens to be a real height discrepancy, in which case only the taller partner does the wrapping. No matter what happens, partners never let go.

Partners face each other with hands clasped. He raises one arm (let's say his L) across his body and up. She turns under it (inside turn) so that her back is to him. He then lowers his raised arm, making a loop in front of her, and she finds herself standing straight jacket style with her back to him. The same arm that was raised to wrap her, raises to unwrap her; and she's back to starting position.

Once you're able to do this turn smoothly under one arm, practice it under the other arm. Then try alternating by wrapping-unwrapping her under the L, then under the R arm. If he's not *too* much taller, she can wrap him under either arm. (Remember that in disco, the guy often does all of the turns). When you combine this turn with a foot pattern, try to complete one wrap-unwrap turn for every 6 count (or 4 count) foot pattern. Later, you'll be able to accomplish *two* of these turns in just 4-6 counts. Or you might decide to abandon the footwork and wrap-unwrap each other several times in a row with all the speed you can muster.

6. WRAP-AND-DUCK TURN

This is a wrap-unwrap turn with a surprise ending.

Partners face each other and hold hands (and never let go). He wraps her up as in the last turn: she passes half way under his L arm (inside turn), and once her back is to him, he drops his L arm in front of her.

Instead of unwrapping her, she pulls a little disappearing act. She "ducks" under his arms (that are crossed in front of her) by bending down and backing up a bit to either his R or L side (doesn't matter which side).

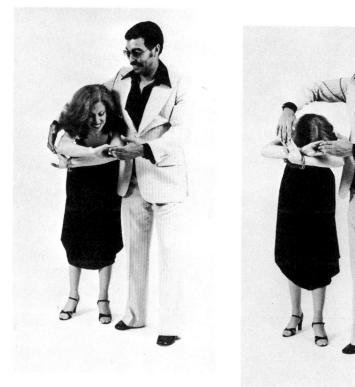

When she straightens up, partners should be facing each other with hands crossed. Without letting go, partners raise both arms, *he turns under them,* and everything is back to normal. There's only one direction he can turn to uncross his arms. If he perchance chooses the *wrong* direction, he breaks his wrists.

Then he attempts the wrap-and-duck turn. Abandon the foot pattern and alternate wrapping and ducking with each other.

7. THE DRAPE (DISHWRAP)

Borrowed from the Jitterbug, this is one popular way that partners arrive at a "crossed hands" position without losing touch with each other.

Partners begin in "open" position (facing each other holding hands), raise both arms high overhead, and move side by side. Now each drops (or "drapes") their clasped hands behind each other's neck, so that one arm is bent with hands clasped behind your own neck; and the other arm is stretched straight with hands clasped behind your partner's neck.

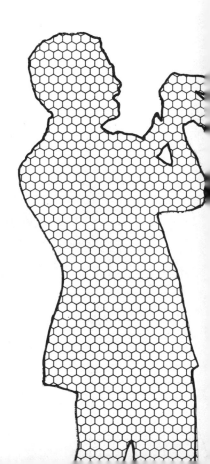

From here, release and drop the hand that's behind your own neck, and let the other hand (the one that's behind your partner's neck) slide down your partner's arm until hands meet and clasp! While your hand slivers down your partner's arm, you're also moving a bit apart from each other. You should now be facing each other with one set of hands crossed, and ready to do some cross-handed turns.

8. CROSSED TWIRL

This turn is done with hands criss-crossed. You may precede it with the Drape, or with any other method of your own creation that has you facing your partner with your R hands clasped and your L hands held (gently) below or above the R set.

From this criss-cross hand position, both of you raise your crossed arms and one of you (doesn't matter who) twirls under them. There's only one way to turn, and you *will* figure it out in no time. After one of you comes out of the twirl, the other immediately follows suit. You could say that you're literally taking turns double crossing each other.

You may prefer to hold the crossed arms together and turn under them at once, or you make like to separate the arms a bit and turn under them individually. It's your choice. This alternate twirling could go on and on until you begin to feel dizzy. Then it's time to stop this turn and try another while your hands are still crossed... maybe the Tango turn coming up next.

9. TANGO TURN

This is a tricky turn with salsa style, so pay close attention. Face each other and clasp hands criss-cross style with L hands on top. *Partners raise their L arms and she turns half way under* then scoots over to his R side (so that you're both standing side by side facing the same direction). Her R arm is "pinned" behind her waist (elbow bent), by his R hand, and both partners have their L arms extended out to the L side "tango" style. If you like you can even dance in this position (he dancing backward while she dances forward or vice-versa).

Now to get out of the tango position, he raises his L arm and she turns under it to face him, hands criss-crossed the way you began.

Whatever you do on one side, you can do on the other! Criss-cross your hands, this time with the R hands on top. Raise your R arms. She turns half way under, and scoots next to his L side. Her L arm is pinned behind her waist by his L hand, and both of you have your R arms extended out to the side. If you like, you may dance one of the foot patterns in a circle (he moves backward, she moves forward or vice-versa) in this tango position. Then he raises his R arm and she turns under it to face him in starting position.

Of course the guy can also do the tango turn by following in her footsteps, so to speak. Then you and your partner can abandon the foot pattern and smoothly alternate the tango (when one comes out of it, the other goes into it). That's when it looks its Latin best.

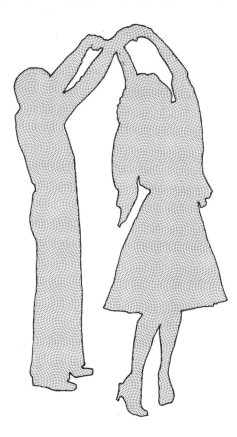

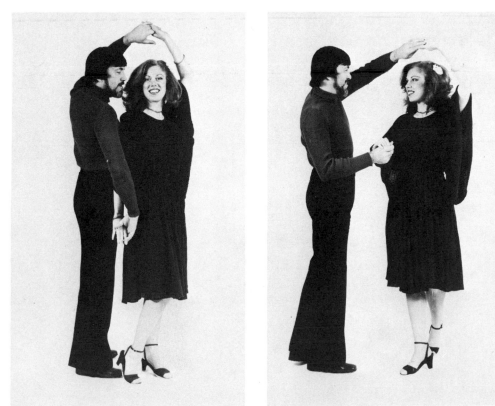

125   *PARTNER DISCO DANCES*

10. THE ROPE

The "Rope" or "Rope Hustle" refers to a certain way the arms are used when dancing any of the 6 count Latin Hustles. There are several ways of "roping"; here are two of the most common ways that go with the Latin-Swing Hustle. I'd advise you to practice the rope arm movements separately from the foot pattern, then combine them.

Partners face each other and hold hands.

A. BASIC ROPE

Counts	Description
1 \} 2 \}	Swing one set of arms out to side
3 \} and \}	Swing them in and up from bent elbows.
4	Swing them slightly down in front of your body.
5	Repeat counts "3 and".
6	Swing arms down and repeat from count 1.

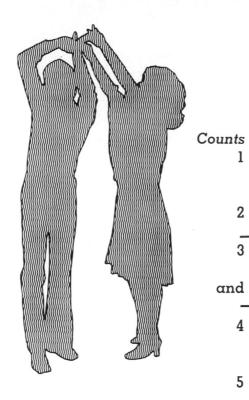

B. DOUBLE DUTCH

Counts	Description
1	Swing both sets of arms out to sides
2	Hold arms sideways
3 and	Describe an inside circle with one set of arms (up around toward center, and down)
4	Describe an inside circle with other set of arms
5	Repeat arms in count "3 and"
6	Leave arms down

ABOUT THE AUTHOR

Karen Lustgarten pioneered disco dance instruction in 1973, and conducts the most popular disco classes on the West Coast. She is also a fitness expert, writes a nationally syndicated newspaper column on exercise, and has written an exercise book on the Lustgarten Technique. Karen was nominated for a Northern California Emmy Award for the exercise and disco dance segments that she wrote, produced, and performed for San Francisco television. Presently she is making plans to open her own entertainment-fitness complex in San Francisco to be called "The Lustgarten."